Initia Sacra: Or Instruction In The Doctrine And Constitution Of The Church Of England

Geldart John E. Riadore

In the interest of creating a more extensive selection of rare historical book reprints, we have chosen to reproduce this title even though it may possibly have occasional imperfections such as missing and blurred pages, missing text, poor pictures, markings, dark backgrounds and other reproduction issues beyond our control. Because this work is culturally important, we have made it available as a part of our commitment to protecting, preserving and promoting the world's literature. Thank you for your understanding.

Initia Sacra:

OR

INSTRUCTION IN THE DOCTRINE AND CONSTITUTION

OF THE

CHURCH OF ENGLAND;

TO WHICH IS ADDED A

SYNOPSIS OF ECCLESIASTICAL HISTORY.

BY THE

REV. GELDART J. E. RIADORE,

B. A., CANTAB, LATE WARDEN OF THE HOUSE OF CHARITY, LONDON,
DOMESTIC CHAPLAIN TO THE DUKE OF BUCCLEUCH AND QUEENSBERRY, K.G.

LONDON:
RIVINGTONS, WATERLOO PLACE.

MDCCCLIX.

A. & W. R. WILSON, PRINTERS, EDINBURGH.

BODLEIAN BIBLIOTHECA

PART I.

CHAPTER I.

THE CHURCH.

Q. 1. To what Church do you belong?

A. To that branch of the Holy Catholic or universal body of Christ's members called the Church of England.

Q. 2. Where do you find an authorised exhibition of its doctrines?

A. In the Creeds, and the Thirty-nine Articles and Prayer Book generally.

Q. 3. Why is this church called the Church of England?

A. Because it is recognised as such by the civil power; and because it is a constant and marked protest against usurpation of her rights and titles by any Christian community setting up in opposition to her.

Q. 4. What do you understand by the catholic church of Christ?

A. The words of the 19th Article of our Church are sufficiently broad; but perhaps the definition of any particular church may be resolved into two or more individuals united in the three Creeds, and living under apostolical succession.

Q. 5. What is the derivation of the word church?

A. It is derived from a Greek word *ecclesia*, an assembly of the faithful. The additional epithet catholic

was not known to the primitive church. Justinian first
ordered the word to be applied to all Christians receiving the Nicene Creed, at the same time commanding
every person and people of the empire to be called
Roman. From which elementary idea, the usurpation
of Rome must advance every theory.

Q. 6. Is the church visible and invisible?

A. Yes. The visible is the congregation of the
faithful; the invisible is that of the just made perfect.

Q. 7. How are we to regard different communions
of Christians?

A. The Catholic Church includes all in her definition if they have been baptized. If they deny her,
they cannot deny the responsibility they had then.
Whatever they observe that is taught by the Church,
so far they are of the Church as far as known and
recognised by such characteristics. They are to be
pitied as denying to themselves the blessings which
full communion with the Church brings with it.

Q. 8. If the doctrines they teach are such as to be
totally inconsistent with the three Creeds, in what
light are they to be looked upon?—Col. i. 18.

A. As heretics.

Q. 9. Who are schismatics?

A. Those guilty of separating from the Church
government.

Q. 10. In what sense is Christ the Head of the Invisible Church?—Eph. i. 21, 22.

A. He is the Lord of those who have departed this
life in His faith and fear, whose good examples we
have to follow, considering the end of their conversation. It is His body that filleth all in all.

Q. 11. How is the Church visible?

A. By her members, government, duties, discipline, and ordinances.

Tertullian an African Father, calls Christ the head of the faithful, in the form of the word Church, *Christus Ecclesia Veri.—(De pœnit :* p. 302*)*.

Q. 12. How is a Church visible in its "Catholicity?"—Eph. iv. 11, 13.

A. If, as in the Church, for fifteen hundred years, Episcopacy be the method of rule.

Q. 13. How in its "antiquity?"

A. Episcopacy is as old as the apostolic institution.

Q. 14. How in "duration?"

A. Episcopal government is divine, and, therefore, has lasted, and apparently will last.

Q. 15. How in "amplitude?"

A. Episcopacy was the sole form of government over the Roman empire.

Q. 16. How is a Church visible by "Consent?"

A. The Church of England agrees with the customs of the first three centuries, and the conclusions of the four great councils.

Q. 17. How in "unity" with Christ as the Head?

A. The Churches Episcopal have never differed from each other since the reformation, in matters of moment or salvation.

Q. 18. How in apostolic doctrine?

A. The few pure doctrines entirely resting on the Bible, and received by the entire early Church, are jealously guarded by the Church of England, in her Creed, Liturgies, and Articles.

Q. 19. How in general reception?

A. The Doctrines and Articles of the Church of

England, are either the foundations of all those Churches which have arisen from her in her colonies, or are received in general as the credenda of the pure faith, by Churches and all christian communities.

Q. 20. How in " holiness ?"

A. The lives of her martyrs, bishops, pastors, and confessors shew this.

Q. 21. How in Prophecies?

A. Sermons on prophecies have ever been greatly honoured means of grace in the Anglican Church.

Q. 22. How in confession of adversaries?

A. It is a remarkable fact that all sects and conditions of men have, in their fiercest vein, universally given credit to the Church of England as *next* to their own, which is a great and wonderful test of its merits,—a homage paid from human vanity.

Q. 23. Is temporal prosperity a visible mark necessary?

A. No. Inward peace and external suffering are more likely to be so. When in the middle ages the Roman See taught as a divine right, the doctrine of its supreme authority, which had never existed in the primitive Church in the remotest sense,—thenceforward the power of Rome descended.

Q. 24. How is Christ the chief and head of this visible Church?

A. He is the author and finisher of the faith visible here on earth in all her members.

Q. 25. What is the meaning of the words, " The head of every man is Christ?"—1 Cor. xi. 3.

A. That every man is bound to regard the Saviour as the sole fountain to him of every individual grace and assistance. This also allows a man to strive to comprehend, with all saints, the love of God, that passeth understanding. He is bound to try the spirits whether they are of God, by previously revealed or previously decided truth. This private judgment, so far as sanctioned by the Church in England, is involved in the Headship of Christ.

Q. 26. Does not this countenance private judgment?

A. Private judgment is and must be exercised. In the Church of Rome, for instance, hesitation in believing everything an ignorant priest might say, would be "private judgment," and must be exercised frequently in Ireland or in Naples. To think conscientiously, and to discriminate between private teaching of a priest and church doctrine as propounded by a synod, is private judgment. A Unitarian would not think it right for a man to deny the moral code laid down in the sermon on the Mount. Judgment is only lawful in subordination to God's fixed laws—beyond that it is nonsense.

Q. 27. Our Lord said to St Peter, "on this rock will I build my Church,"—What did He mean?

A. He alluded to the foundation which was fulfilled on the day of Pentecost, when St Peter converted the first 3000 souls to Christ. St Peter is not foretold to be the head, but the "foundation."

Q. 28. Is Christ the head of the nations?—Rev. i. 5; xix. 16.

A. Yes, as He is Prince of the kings of the earth. Therefore it is evil and sinful to deny in a christian country, that the government thereof has any necessary connexion with the national religion.

Q. 29. What did our Lord mean by the words, "one is your Master?—S. Matt. xxiii. 8, 9.

A. That they should not exercise supreme authority over each other.

Q. 30. Are there instances which show to us, from the history of nations, that God has regard to those who, in their executive capacity, support or degrade the Church by national sin?—Is. xiv. 21; Jer. ii. 2-7; Dan. viii. 23; Rev. ii. 4, 5.

A. Yes. Israel was punished in the days of David for sins contracted 400 years before; and the Jews, in the time of our Saviour, came under denunciations prophesied of Moses before his death. Nor does this rule obtain only with the Jewish nations, but with the Persian, Babylonian, and Grecian Empires.

Q. 31. Is the Church held responsible for error and strange doctrine? And, if so, what is the deduction? —2 Thess. i. 2; 1 Cor. i.; Gal. iii.; Rev. ii. 3.

A. Assuredly. The Church of Corinth is addressed in its collective capacity, and rebuked for schism. The Galatian Church rebuked for a disposition to rest upon obsolete ordinances of the Jewish Church. The Churches of Ephesus, Sardis, Philadelphia, Laodicœa, are rebuked and praised in the person of the bishops of each. One especially is praised for holding fast the faith, and judiciously casting out the Nicolaitan heresy. The deduction is, that the Church teaches what is truth and defines what is not, and also hath authority in matters of rites and ceremonies.

Q. 32. If the civil power refuse aid in carrying out her denouncement and punishment, what resource has she?

A. None. She can execute her final punishment of excommunication, and that alone. For the rest, she saveth her own conscience, and waits patiently in the Lord.

Q. 33. Is there any mention of rites and ceremonies, and matters of faith, settled by the Church in apostolic times?—Acts iv. 34, vi. 1 ; viii. 5, 14.

A. Yes. The Lord's day, arrangement by the Church of property voluntarily left to it by members, the appointment of deacons, the first decision of the necessity of articles of faith, to abstain from meats offered to idols, &c., confirmation, &c.

Q. 34. Did our Lord allow the Jewish Church the right of alteration in matters which had apparently been settled by Mosaical command?

A. Yes. For instance, our Lord sat down after the Greek custom, or rather reclined at the Passover, when by the law, all were to eat it standing.

Q. 35. Does this show that the Church has power to ordain and to abrogate non-essentials.

A. Yes.

Q. 36. Did our Lord give any guide in this matter? S. Math. xviii. 17.

A. Scarcely any, beyond one important command to hear the Church; and that a refractory member, refusing to obey the Church, was to be in the eyes of the rest of the brethren a heathen.

Q. 37. Did our Lord ordain any ordinance but Baptism and the Holy Eucharist?

A. No. The Lord's Day as a weekly festival, infant baptism, episcopal ordination, confirmation, most undoubtedly arose from the Church apostolic, and have been continued from the earliest times.

Q. 38. Many churches have erred in these matters, and yet maintain essential marks of a church?

A. The marks of a church are apostles' doctrine, and unity, breaking of bread, and common prayer as mentioned in Acts ii. v. 42. And churches have erred; as anciently the Church of Jerusalem or Antioch erred, so the Church of Rome hath erred in ceremonies and in faith, and yet is a branch of the one Catholic Church.

Q. 39. Can a branch of the Catholic Church purify herself from errors formerly acknowledged?

A. Yes, and must do so. "Repent," says the angel to the erring Church of Pergamos, Rev. ii, 12-14. Our bishops met and said there are errors which, however they may have been held under bondage to the Bishop of Rome, we are bound to renounce in this realm of England. For the first ten years after this, there was but one communion in the Church of England, till the Pope fulminated anathemas against the person of Elizabeth.

Q. 40. If the Church is thus armed with authority to teach, and is the body of Christ—is it wrong to deny her teaching?

A. Yes. Though there is a limit to her teaching, so that she cannot enforce anything contrary to her office of witness and keeper only of Holy Writ.

Q. 41. On what grounds might private judgment be exercised in troublous and perilous times.

A. "If the foundations are cast down, what hath the righteous done?" Faith and humble patience will lead all to rest, in God's good time. We have one certain text to strengthen us, given by St Paul, "Though I an angel," &c.

Q. 42. Are the interpretations of Sacred Scripture,

which are given by the priests of the Church, to be received as the teaching of Christ?

A. Only so far as agreeing with all Scripture, and blessed with Christ's grace as an ordinance.

Q. 43. Did the Church very early require certain definitions of orthodoxy?

A. Yes. As mentioned above. (Quest. 33.)

Q. 44. Why?

A. As exhibitions against error, tests of communion, means of instruction, helps for understanding.

Q. 45. In what way might an individual justly suspect the teaching of the Church?

A. When, as before the Reformation, the functions that relate to the bestowal of offices, and the dispensation of ordinances, in doctrine, worship, discipline, and government, are directed under a single bishop; and, moreover, not in conformity to those laws which Jesus has Himself prescribed.

Q. 46. What four great liturgies were in use during the fourth century?

A. At the end of the fourth century the oriental liturgy prevailed from the Euphrates to the Hellespont and to the south of Greece. The Alexandrian, which was the liturgy of Egypt, Abyssinia, and the country inland towards the west, along the Mediterranean Sea. The Roman, which prevailed through Italy, Sicily, and the civil diocese of Africa. The fourth was the Gallican, which prevailed through Gaul and Spain.

Q. 47. Did the early British Church lean to the Eastern custom in some particulars?

A. Yes. When Austin came to England, he wished to persuade the British Church to change their observance of Easter to the western rule.

Q. 48. Why?

A. Because the British Church obtained her liturgical and ritual customs from the East.

Q. 49. Explain?

A. The Christians in Gaul derived their conversion from Arabic converts, and the Church at Lyons was the origin of the Gallic Church, which was in constant communion with the British, before they were conquered by the Saxon barbarians.

Q. 50. Did Austin succeed?

A. Yes. By threatening the British Church with war if they did not yield.—(*Bede Historia, lib.* 1.)

Q. 51. Was the liturgy corrupted?

A. Yes. The missal of Osmond, arch-bishop of Canterbury in the eleventh century, was five times the size of the primitive liturgies to which the Church returned at the reformation.

Q. 52. Give some services not in the Sacramentary of Gregory, but afterwards added to the Roman service.

A. 1. Litanies to the Virgin,—tenth century.

2. Canonization of Saints,—seventh century.

3. Invocation of Angels,—prohibited by the Council of Laodicea in the fourth century, restored in the seventh.

Q. 53. What remarkable analogy is there between the Roman and Anglican communion service?

A. In the fact, that recitation of the words of institution is all that is required for valid consecration.

Q. 54. How?

A. Because the rubric directs in the case of insufficient quantity of the holy elements, the repetition only of that portion of the service which includes the words of instituiton.

Q. 55. What does this prove?

A. It proves that equally Rome and the Anglican Churches do not follow all antiquity.

Q. 56. Does the Greek Church?

A. Yes. It has invocation, oblation, and institution,—which all antiquity ever had.

Q. 57. But is there no mention of oblations?

A. Yes. We conclude a valid oblation is supposed in the words in Church militant prayer, " our oblations, which we offer, &c."

Q. 58. Does our consecration prayer include invoeation?

A. Yes it does. And so far we are more catholic and correct than Rome. And though badly arranged and displaced, yet, there is in the whole service, implied and mentioned, the three essences of valid consecration, rehearsal of words of institution; oblation of elements; and invocation of the Holy Spirit.

Q. 59. How many forms of absolution are used in our offices; and do they necessitate private confessions *as required* acts?

A. Three. Private confession as appears from Tertullian, was never required as a constant act of discipline in the early Church, and is not required by ours.

Q. 60. What is the voice of our Church?

A. The voice of our Church is plain, and to that voice we must give heed, whether it be agreeable to primitive antiquity or not. If "the conscience is troubled with any weighty manner," *before Holy Communion*, then imparting that secret or those secret sins, is ordered by the Church of England, to a priest, and he is to give absolution.

Q. 61. But although absolution and confession are doctrines of the Church of England, as they are of all Catholic Churches, how has she wisely acted in limitation thereof?

A. In so far as the constant regulation of any man's life, is not an injurious sacrifice of personal and christian liberty.

Q. 62. Is a true remission of sins conveyed in the absolution of the morning service?

A. Yes, undoubtedly. To such as are fit for it, a remission, not necessarily intelligible as to amount or the nature of sins remitted, is conveyed in precisely the same manner as the words of the Saviour, "thy sins be forgiven thee," would convey no distinct idea of what sins, or as the "Peace" to this house of the Apostles on being sent forth by their Master, was not defined or explicable minutely to those who were in a state to receive it.

PART II.

CHAPTER II.

AUTHORITY OF THE CHURCH.

Q. 63. Are the laws of Christ, as in the Bible, sufficient for all purposes of church government?

A. The principles and directions contained in the New Testament, though sufficient for an elementary

Church, yet the historical system, which conveys the Church's experience and judgment, and those deep mysteries which are wont to be accepted as the catholic faith, must act in a co-relative though subordinate authority with Sacred Writ.

Q. 64. If by peculiar circumstances a church is connected with the State, and consequently deplores much irregularity, is that a sufficient reason to judge her?

A. No. The assumption of church prerogative by the civil power is one of the drawbacks of the Church being connected with the State. There is no resource beyond meek endurance and patiently waiting in the Lord.

Q. 65. Is it a grievance that the Church has no convocation, no voice in the election of bishops, in increasing or diminishing them, and in the general ecclesiastical wants of the age?

A. Yes. The government of the Church pertains to the portion of it that represents its authority, and it is her misfortune rather than her fault, that she is constrained to endure what she constantly protests against.

Q. 66. Yet is the State to have no voice in spiritual things?—1 Chron. xxix. 22, 23; 2 Chron. xviii. 4-6; 2 Kings iii. 11.

A. Yes. David, Jehoshaphat, and Hezekiah, took part in the restoration and regulation of the Church of Israel. But certainly not without consideration of the opinions of those whose authority in the Church is undoubted, such as bishops and presbyters. St. Paul appealed to Cæsar.

Q. 67. Was Saul the head of the Jewish Church in a civil or political sense?

A. He was called the head of the tribes of Israel, to see that all things were managed for that great and architectional end: that is, the weal and benefit of the whole body politic, both for soul and body.* The king is," says Bishop Jeremy Taylor, "supreme of the jurisdiction, that part of it which is the external compulsory.

Q. 68. Is there any proof to be gathered that this was ever the law of England before the Pope of Rome caused a schism in the Church?

A. Yes. The Constitutions of Clarendon, say,— "When an appeal came to the king from the archbishop, he was not to take cognizance of the cause himself, but was to provide that justice be done in the court of the arch-bishop, and the appeal not carried further (to Rome) without the KING's *consent.*

Q. 69. Can you give any instance of the unreal character of the jurisdiction claimed by Rome.

A. Yes. Although a few years previously she anathematised Queen Elizabeth, Rome quietly subscribed to an arbitrary restoration of her errors in faith and practice, brought about on the accession of Mary, although it was by the Queen's sole authority, and not that of Rome.

Q. 70. Whenever undue pressure is exercised by the State, is that any reason for abusing the Church as the author of things over which she has no control? or does that give any grounds for judging her?

A. None. A true church person will find in all such occasions, only calls to submission and patience, and an opportunity to offer up their own wishes and wills to God.

* See Bramhall's Works, answer to M. de la Militière, p. 25.

Q. 71. What then ought the State to do?

A. To agree to a covenant of friendship, co-operation, and assistance.

Q. 72. Did the influence of the king over the Jewish Church always secure good?

A. No. In the kingdom of Israel the dynasties were changed ten times; nine were extirpated because they had made Israel to sin.

Q. 73. Is this the way in which a country may be punished now for similar sin?

A. Yes.

Q. 74. Was the case the same in Judah?

A. No. The dynasties lasted for nineteen successions in the *line* of David, nevertheless the cause of destruction was national sin in that the people disregarded God.

Q. 75. If the increasing latitudinarian views of the times at last effect a disjunction of Church and State, what would result?

A. That as an establishment, the Church, in that aspect, would suffer much temporal loss. The government would suffer, and the State in general would suffer greatly, and the Crown not less so.

Q. 76. But is the Crown responsible for the acts of the State?

A. No. Therefore, in this country, the Crown would probably not suffer the punishments which history tells us are manifested in the Bourbon families— exile and dethronement.

Q. 77. Is it likely that a government that apostatized from the Church, alienated her property, and destroyed as much as possible her prestige could exist long?

A. Not as the government of a first-rate nation. Antichrist will then sit in the palaces as well as the temples of the land.

Q. 78. Is there any difference worthy of remark in the way in which successors to apostolic and inferior offices were elected?

A. Yes. The apostles were chosen from their own body. They alone admitted the deacons to their duties.

Q. 79. Was this system continued?

A. Yes. With some modification, as we may judge from the Epistles of St Paul to Timothy and Titus.

Q. 80. Was it necessary that human authority should seal the Divine mission?

A. Yes. As our Saviour was baptized and declared the ordinance necessary to fulfil all righteousness, so in the same spirit the Holy Ghost said " separate me Barnabas and Saul.".

Q. 81. What did " Separate me " imply?

A. It implied imposition of hands of the apostles and presbyters; with prayer and fasting.

Q. 82. What does this imply with regard to those who have no authority, yet style themselves ambassadors of God?

A. They do so on their own responsibility. But any one of the hearers of such teachers has as much right to declare to him as he to them.

Q. 83. Were deacons ordained with the same power and authority as the presbyter?—Acts viii. 5-12; xI. 19, 20.

A. Certainly not. A deacon might exercise other duties of lay character, and still preach, and even baptize as Philip; some were not even deacons as Apollos, and those scattered abroad after the death of Stephen.

Q. 84. Does the Church of England agree with this?

A. Yes—entirely. Scripture readers, schoolmasters, captains of ships, may instruct in Christ, and preach Him crucified, but they may not arrogate to themselves priestly offices.

85. Does the Church of England proceed in her ordination regulations after the model of the Early Church?

A. Yes. With no greater difference than there was between the church custom in the apostle's time, and in the time of Timothy and Titus and their successors.

86. Are the candidates taken from the people?

A. Yes. And any person can, if he give sufficient reason, prevent ordination.

Q. 87. What is to be gathered from the account in Mark ix. 38?

A. That no one was forbidden casting out devils in Christ's name, because simply he was not a follower of Christ.

Q. 88. Can any argument in favour of dissenting teachers having authority and lawful ministry, be deduced from it?

A. None. For the man was not even a Christian; and it had reference to a gift long ceased to the Christian Church itself.

Q. 89. May nevertheless God's blessing be upon a congregation and self-appointed minister?

A. It may be so. But it is a remarkable fact that, when our Lord wished to silence the Pharisees, he said

B

of the baptism of John, is it of heaven or of men?
Again, in the Early Church after the apostolic age,
parties who seceded from any branch of the Church,
always attempted to gather together under some bishop
or pseudo-bishop.

In any branch of the Church salvation is lost by the
member's deficiencies; but in schismatic bodies of
Christians, there is a possibility of all ordinances being
uncovenanted, unauthorised, and useless.

It must be to such also that the warning cry of our
Saviour was addressed, "Go not after them, nor follow them."

Q. 90. Does the character of an individual invalidate
authority duly received?

A. No. As the apostleship of Judas and his minis-
terial acts to those who received him, were as valid as
the acts of the rest of the apostles.

Q. 91. But are there no characteristics which should
be evident in ministers of Christ?

A. Yes. They are plainly set forth in 1 Tim. iii.
1-12, and in Tit. i. 5-9.

Q. 92. Is there anything there given which would fairly
intimate a difference between presbyters and deacons
such as obtains in all branches of the Catholic Church?

A. Yes. The superior officer termed bishop, elected
from the presbyters, was called to rule, and direction
given that he should not be a novice, lest he might be
lifted up with pride of distinction. That he was to
command and to teach doctrines. That he was to
rule elders, and to have over them the authority of
a father over a child, and to be careful in receiving
accusations against elders, which, of course, inferenced
the episcopal power of judgment.

Q. 93. When may we ordinarily conclude that one is answering faithfully the first questions directed to deacons in the Ordination Service of the Church of England?

A. When he finds reason to conclude that zeal and love to souls incline him to the work, and when the Church is prepared to recognise him.

Q. 94. Does any congregation have it in their power to refuse a *candidate?*

A. Yes; at the reading of the " Si quis." *

Q. 95. If a clerk, officiating as assistant-curate in a parish, should offend, can he be displaced by his incumbent?

A. Not if licensed by the bishop. Only by withdrawal of the bishop's license can such an one be removed. The Church does not recognise an unlicensed clerk.

Q. 96. What are sides men, synod's men, or quest men?

A. Persons appointed to assist church-wardens in their duties. In ancient episcopal synods, they gave evidence against irregularities of the clergy, as well as against heretics. By Canon 90, they were to be chosen at Easter.

Q. 97. What is the difference between rectories, vicarages, and incumbencies, or perpetual curacies?

A. Rectories are when the predial tithes are in the hands of the parson. If impropriated in lay hands, or appropriated in some ecclesiastical communion, then the parson is the *vicar.* Perpetual curacy is a modern term which implies that the cure of souls is entirely in

* " Si quis," from the first two words of the challenge or notice to the parish, bound to be given by a candidate for ordination.

the hands of the parson; but it may be without encroaching upon the rights of the parish church.

Q. 98. What is meant by a title to orders?

A. By the Canons of 1603, a bishop must support at his charges *an admitted candidate for orders till* his preferment to duty with stipend, unless the bishop receives proof that he has " a title," either by a fellowship in a college or as a chaplain, or as a master of arts of five years' standing, or *the promise of employment by rector or vicar.*

Q. 99. What is the authority of a dean?

A. The word dean is derived from a Greek word meaning ten, as presiding over ten or more canons. When Henry VIII. suppressed the convents and abbots, they were changed into deans and chapters. The new foundations were those instituted by Henry. The old foundations call on the chapter to elect a dean, subject to the *conge d' elire* of the king, the bishops confirming. The new foundations are subject to shorter process and are donative, the dean being installed by king's letters patent, the letters patent being presented by the bishop for institution. These dignities are filled up by the king if void by consecration of the previous holder to a bishopric. The bishops only of St David and Llandaff are supreme head in their respective chapters. They have powers generally independant and dependant with regard to the bishop.

Q. 100. What is a rural dean?

A. Formerly one who had a district of ten churches or parishes in town or country over which he exercised jurisdiction. At first they were called *archipresbyteri*, and were supreme to archdeacons. At first elected by the clergy, afterwards removeable and elected by the bishop, and called *Decani Temporarii* to distinguish them from the perpetual deans of cathedrals. They inquired into dilapidation, examined candidates for confirmation, and exercised other inferior jurisdiction.

PART III.

CHAPTER III.

POWER OF THE KEYS.

Q. 101. In what way has the Church power?

A. In and by the power of the keys, by absolution; also in doctrine, rites, and discipline—Matt. xvi. 19; Acts xv.; 1 Cor. xiv. 26-40; Acts xx.; Matt. xviii. 18.

Q. 102. Describe the absolving power.

A. There are three forms in the Church of England, and its branches all over the world. "The voice is man's voice, which pronounces this absolution, but it is the indwelling power of our great High-priest which pardons the penitent. Christ has given this, His own power, to man. He hath conferred this power, and hath given authority to those who truly are priests to execute in His stead. There is in truth only one Priest, that is, Christ the Lord, and they who are called priests are so only as representing Him who abideth a priest for ever, and as doing what He has ordained them to perform. As in the absolution, so in the consecration of bread and wine. It is still the priestly power of Christ which makes the bread His body to us and the wine His blood. That power which He possessed in the upper room of Jerusalem on the night he was betrayed, He still continues to exercise."

Q. 103. When is the dogmatic power abused?

A. When the Church decrees aught against the Holy Scriptures, and enforces beside it anything to be believed as of necessity to salvation.

Q. 104. If the Church is the pillar and ground of the truth, it is required to put implicit faith in it, is it not?.

A. Yes. To the extent limited only by the twenty-first article of our Church. It is infallible to the extent of its being a witness and keeper of Holy Writ —for if any one Christian writes down what is to be believed as necessary to be saved according to the Gospel, that, of course, is infallible, and that the Church is the keeper of and witness to.

Q. 105. But the Church may err nevertheless?

A. Yes. When she proceeds beyond her authority.

Q. 106. What is the great deficiency in the authority of a sect?

A. That it never can have the same force and obligation as that authority which has been consecrated by ages of agreement and in all parts and by all. The authority of private interpretation cannot be equal to the authority, erudition, and learning of many.

Q. 106. What is the natural tendency of minds brought up without due and reasonable consideration of the Church as a Divine institution?

A. In times of rest and fullness, perhaps little is thought about it at all ; but in times of reaction and revival, the tendency must be to unbelief, or to believe without reasonable limits, as after excitement or distraction, any decision which gets rid of personal responsibility is anxiously looked for. For that, Rome answers at all hazards; and various sectarian communities of Christians provide for tones of thought opposed to all Catholic ideas and aspects of truth.

Q. 107. On what grounds does the Anglican Church *not differ* from the Romish Church?

A. In expressions of reverence, or of the more enthusiastic feelings in devotional exercise, common to both in ritual or ceremony. Much may be common to both, and much should be; but it is the fault of puritanism to see in any tendency towards a glorious and splendid ritual, a mark only of opposition to the "Gospel."

Q. 108. Is this not a denial of Christian liberty?

A. Yes, decidedly. Our Church has provided in her ritual for the simplest, as well as for the more expressive forms of reverence, according as the earnestness and feelings of the congregation may desire. Our protest against Rome is independent of such matters, and rests on a return to primitive doctrine and government only, and on no other ground whatever. It is the awful ignorance in these things which has made sects and schisms.

Q. 109. But if the Church of England is wearied with many sects, is not that an argument against her?

A. No. There never has been a time when uniformity has existed in the Visible Church, or any branch of it.

Q. 110. Rome is an exception, is it not?

A. Least of all. She desires to compromise for appearance when weak, or to be cruel when she is strong, as in the time of the Inquisition, forgetful of the fact, that its very existence proved the wide spreading of the evil it professed to destroy,

Q. 111. Does the Church of England then connive at the sects without her?

A. No. But she has no authority in sacred Scripture to kill and destroy those who forsake her. They are judged by one in Heaven. Schism is an evil, and is admitted as an evil of the Visible Church. In its visible character, it partakes of the natural infirmity common to humanity.

Q. 112. Have there been disputes in the Roman Church?

A. Yes. Between Popes and Anti-Popes. The great schism of the west in 1378–1415. Quarrels between the different orders of Regulars, Bishops, and Monks, Gallicans and Ultramontanes.

Q. 113. What is the great difference then?

A. Simply that Rome compromises for appearance, and the Anglican Church neither condemns nor judges, but ignores sects.

Q. 114. But are there not great differences within her?

Yes. Schools of Divinity will always exist. But they must exist in a free country. Roman Catholicism would not exist in France, but for a concordat; and when an enforced subjection to authority exists, there also is secret or open infidelity and rebellion. The practical faults and errors of the Anglican Church may be deplored; but those of Rome are far greater and more soul-ensnaring.

Q. 116. Does the national character have any influence in the development of church principles?

A. Yes. Great love of liberty and exercise of it makes it impossible to accept as much error with the truth as Rome is able to induce the southern nations to accept.

Q. 117. What do you mean by "the truth" as a general expression?

A. Apostle's doctrine and fellowship, as manifested by the Catholic creeds, sacraments, and apostolical orders.

Q. 118. If so, ought we not to communicate with foreign churches when we are abroad?

A. The only ground of not receiving the communion in the church of the country in which we are, is the ground of its involving an act of sin.

Q. 119. What is then the duty of a sincere Roman Catholic, or Anglican Churchman, under all trials and obstacles?

A. To cling more closely to their particular branch of the Church, and, as far as possible, by prayer and meek behaviour, live an ensample to all them that are without.

Divisions and schools of divinity are an inseparably attendant upon the truth; and the apostle plainly declares there must be heresies and divisions.

Q. 120. Does not this accord much dangerous scope to individual opinion?

A. Not more than Christian liberty allows. Rational conviction of what is idolatry and error is fully gained from the doctrines and language set forth in the Prayer Book; therefore no sound churchman, although a weak and foolish member, might be induced

grounds communicate in the Greek or Roman Church for instance.

PART IV.

CHAPTER IV.

GOVERNMENT OF THE CHURCH.

Q. 121. What is the difference between the Church and the Establishment?

A. The Church is the spiritual body; the establishment is the statutory provision of tithes, glebe, endowments, or other property of the Church, for the provision thereof.

Q. 122. Is *schism* always inseparable from disjunction from the authority of the Church?

A. No. If the plain teaching of the Bible, the consent of ages, and the adding or taking away from the Word, is abused by the Church, then separation is not schism, for continuance would be sin.

Q. 123. Why so?

A. Agreeably to the words of St Paul (Gal. i. 8), that any other Gospel preached contradictory to *The One*, would be accursed.

Q. 124. What position does the king of these realms hold with reference to the Church?

A. He has the chief power in this realm of England and his other dominions; unto him belongs the chief government of all estates of this realm, whether they be ecclesiastical or civil.

Q. 125. Can you give any sound definition, from an authoritative writer, of the king's supremacy.

A. Dr T. Jackson, who was at Oxford in the time of James I., says, "The truth of a doctrine being resolved by a synod, and the contrary error condemned for heresy, the king, as supreme governor in all cases, hath a coercive power over every worship, to compel them to .censure delinquents." Mason, a writer of equal authority, states, "It belongs to the spiritual pastors, or masters, to explain,—and to kings to publish the truth when it is explained, and to enforce it with his commands upon all his subjects, of what order or condition soever they be." See Mason's Vindication of English Ministry, p. 228. In fact, all that the State does is to put into motion the machinery of the Church.

Q. 126. Is this in some sort the origin of much disorganization.

A. Yes; with certain advantages, it prevents organization and continuation, and places the Church under the arbitrary will of one man—the prime minister —by whom the king really acts.

Q. 127. Is this the most offensive part?

A. Yes. The king really acting as a working Father of the invisible Church would be invaluable.

Q. 128. Has the power of the king, when tyrannically exercised, been ever opposed?

A. Frequently. Especially in the memorable action against the seven bishops in the reign of James II.

Q. 129. In what body is the proper government of Church matters vested?

A. In synods, and more especially in convocation;

and in the theory nothing can be more grand than
that of the British Constitution, when spiritual and
lay are properly represented, and act in unison with
each other for the glory of God. It is the perversion
of the rights of the Church that is the ground of her
complaint and long dissatisfaction.

Q. 135. Are the names of bishops and presbyters
very ancient?

A. Yes. Of the same date as the apostolical
Church. They were appointed to take oversight of
the flock, and also of those who were the spiritual
pastors of the flock. Whether they be called bishops
or overseers is of no consequence.—Philipp. ii. 25.
" Your Apostle."

Q. 136. What reasons from Holy Scripture can
you give in support of this view?

A. From the fact, that to the apostles were added
others who had with them equal authority :

As Paul, Barnabas, James, Bishop of Jerusalem,
mentioned in Galatians (Gal. i. 19. "But other of the
apostles saw I none, save James, &c.") Andronicus
and Junia are mentioned by St Paul as of note *among*
the apostles. Silas is mentioned in the Acts a chief
man among the brethren, and of his own will remains
at Antioch to confirm the Church there. Silas, St
Paul, and Timothy are described as equal in authority ;
and, in 2d Thess. we read the words, "The things
which we command you."—Acts i. 21, 22; xv. 6.
The office might nevertheless, at a very early period,
have been less distinguished than in the latter part of
the first century. It is certain from Scripture that
only those were equal in all things with an apostle,
who had special charge over a church, which is all

that is wanted in thé argument.—Acts xv. 22 ; xxxii.
25, 27, 34; xvi.; Gen. i. 19; 1 Thess. i. 1 ; 2 Thess.
iii. 4, 6, 8, 9. The voice of profane history is quite
certain.—Rom. xvi. 7.

Q. 137. What is metropolitan power?

A. Titus was head bishop or metropolitan of Crete,
and Timothy of proconsular Asia, according to S.
Chrysostom in his fifteenth homily on the first Epistle
to Timothy. In the year 177, Irenæus succeeded
Pothinus, and superintended the Galician provinces,
though he was bishop of Lyons in fact.

Q. 138. Give some instances of archiepiscopal pre-
cedence.

A. The provincial synods towards the end of the
second century, convened to consider the paschal con-
troversy, were presided over by the metropolitan, as
Victor in that of Rome, Irenæus of Lyons in that of
France, Polycrates of Ephesus in that of proconsular
Asia.

Q. 139. Did the death of the apostles destroy the
links of their high office?

A. No. There were already many bishops to ordain
in every branch of the Church.

Q. 140. Were bishops to be considered necessary in
congregations?

A. No. Only when many congregations became a
province as it were for the bishop to superintend.

Q. 141. Did our Lord ordain the orders which the
Church afterwards saw reason to introduce beside the
apostles.

A. No. The appointment of presbyters or elders
is passed over with the briefest notices. In the 11th
chapter of Acts, v. 30, the latter word occurs in an

accidental way, in all other passages nearly, they are spoken of as ordained by apostles, and inferior to them. When entrusted with a pastoral charge, the name of elder and that of bishop was synonymous. But they *never ordained others* but as bishops in that sense only.

Q. 142. Did the early bishops exercise the office any where?

A. Yes. Titus was sometimes exercising episcopal jurisdiction at Corinth as well as in Crete. The diocese of a bishop is a mere accidental part of his official character.

Q. 143. Is there anything remarkable in the words used by St Paul to the effect that he received not his mission from men?

A. Yes. It shows that some, as Matthias, had. But St Paul had received it from the Lord Himself in a mysterious way.

Q. 144. What is remarkable in the messages directed to the seven churches?

A. The angel is addressed as being responsible for the government of the Church. A presbyter presiding among his brethren in superior exercise of rank and power, is what is called a bishop—and this must have been the case, for there is but one person addressed as the angel of the Church, and there must have been many congregations.—Revelation ii. 10, 13, 24, 25. The angels or bishops are addressed in one instance (2nd chapter of Revelations) as renowned for calmness and patience, and for " trying those who say they are apostles, and are not."—Rom. ii. 2.

Q. 145. May any ecclesiastical function be assumed without warrant of Christ through the Church?

A. No. To do so is directly against Scripture, which is very clear upon the subject.—Heb. v. 4.

Q. 146. Would a Moderator of an Assembly of presbyters answer to the apostolic office of overseer or bishop?

A. No. For he only has personally to do with power in the matter of a casting vote among other votes. He counts votes and keeps order, and could not be responsible for the defects and corruption of a church as the angel of the Church of Sardis was.

Q. 147. Does the Church allow of the idea of presbyters?

A. Yes. For instance, in 1 Tim. iv. 14, the college of apostles is intended. But they had received the grace of apostleship. The apostles, in fact, designated themselves presbyters, but they corresponded to bishops, for presbyters did not ordain bishops or presbyters in that sense. Those who would be competent to ordain in the Presbyterian sense held in modern times, had not even power to ordain a deacon. St Paul ascribes the ordination of Timothy to his own act and deed, as the Greek word " διά " so forcibly implies: and when the words laying on of hands of the presbytery occur, we have the word μετὰ, which, in fact, exactly corresponds to the Anglican custom.

Q. 148. But did not the promise, " I am with you to the end of the world," cease with the miraculous power of Apostles?

A. No. For Christ's words would now have had no meaning, unless, after the decease of the apostles, their functions remained eternal, received from Christ as necessary to the order and office of governors of the Church. There is the real presence of God the Holy

Ghost also, equally mysterious, equally inexplicable, equally beyond the power of our intellect to understand; yet St Paul affirms this truth to the Corinthians,— " Know ye not that ye are the temple of God, and that the Spirit of God dwelleth in you?" And again, " What! know ye not that your body is the temple of the Holy Ghost which is in you, which ye have of God?" And these very Corinthians of whom he thus speaks he had previously rebuked for their sins. Who can fathom this wonderful mystery, that God the Holy Ghost dwelleth in the bodies of the regenerate? The infidel may ask, indeed, how can this be? Can the Holy Ghost dwell in more than one body at one and the same time? Our only answer is, God hath spoken it by the mouth of His apostles. It is an article of faith.

Q. 149. The apostles were designated Presbyters you say, were they ever called by other names?

A. Yes. Prophets.—Romans xvi. 25–27; Ephes. iii. 45.

Q. 150. Is the idea of twelve only, as applied to the apostles, correct?

A. No. The term was applied to all elected into the body. As James, Andronicus, and Junia, mentioned by St Paul, as of note, " among the apostles."

Q. 151. How do commentators escape the dilemma in which these facts place the argument against the necessity of apostolic order in the Church?·

A. By calling those beyond the twelve, apostles in a secondary sense, with Neander and others.

Q. 152. Is there any undesigned evidence met with to favour the idea of the Church being episcopal.

A. Yes. Silas, for instance, remaining of his own will

own will at Antioch (Acts xv. 34). In the occurrences at Philippi, he is constantly mentioned as the equal of St Paul.—Acts xvi. See 2 Cor. i. 19 ; 1 Thess. i. 1 ; ii. 6, 8 ; 2 Thess. iii. 4 ; i. 6 ; i. 8, 9.

Q. 153. Mention any other kind of evidence of this nature.

A. Successors of the apostles must have been elected if we find people alluded to as "false apostles," as mentioned by St Paul. Again, St John, who was the sole survivor, mentions those, who say " they are apostles and are not." It only needed for St John to state himself to be the only one left to be implicitly believed ; but, on the contrary, he acknowledged the existence of the apostolic office by calling to notice the false pretenders to its dignity.

Q. 154. Christ then, when breathing on His twelve disciples the Holy Ghost, conferred a transmissive power?

A. Yes. He was to be present with His Church, as it were, in the office, not in the persons of the Twelve. Nothing but a corruption of doctrine can in any way give grounds for separation from episcopal authority, which is the transmitted power of Christ.

Q. 155. Does St Paul ever anticipate the wayward spirit which would suggest opposition to and unbelief in apostolic authority?

A. Yes. In 2 Cor. xii. 12, he says, "Truly the signs of an apostle were wrought among you *in all patience*, in signs, and wonders, and mighty deeds." Apostles therefore needed evidence of their Divine mission even in early periods.

Q. 156. As apostles and prophets were frequently

synonymous terms, when prophets are spoken of, are they apostles or bishops?

A. Neither. Simeon called Niger, Lucius of Cyrene, Mansen and Agabus are spoken of as prophets, but not apostles; Joseph called Barsabas, Stephen, and Philip, who worked miracles, were not apostles; nor did the apostolic office depend upon the individual or accidental accompaniments, but upon consecration.—Acts xiii. 1; xxi. 10; Acts vi. 8; viii. 6.

Q. 157. Is there any instance of irresistible evidence of the ideal of Diocesan superintendence, which, by peculiar interpretation, is apt to be overlooked in our version of the New Testament?

A. Yes. Philippians ii. 25. The words are: "Yet I supposed it necessary to send to you Epaphroditus, my brother, and companion in labour, and fellow-soldier, but your messenger, and he that ministered to my wants." Ἀπόστολος is translated "messenger." The word ought to have been rendered apostle, the ruler, in fact, of the Philippian Church. Otherwise St Paul, who was sent by the Church at Corinth to bring alms and offerings (Acts xxiv. 17), would only have in the same way been worthy of the name "messenger." So also Paul and Barnabas going to Jerusalem as "messengers" from Antioch.

Q. 158. Is there any other passage where the similar evasion of the force attached to the word apostle is avoided?

A. Yes; one only (2 Cor. viii. 23), where the word "messengers" is evidently forced. They were bishops elect—a glory of Christ. The translators wished to avoid, it may be supposed, any reflection upon those communities of Christians which were represented in non-episcopal governments.—See Stanley's Corinthians, vol. ii. p. 166.

PART V.

CHAPTER V.

JUDICATORIES OF THE CHURCH.

Q. 159. To whom does the government of a congregation, and aggregate congregations or churches, belong?

A. To the spiritual masters and pastors.—Matt. xvi. 19; Eph. iv. 11; 1 Cor. xii. 28; Tit. i. 7.

Q. 160. Why do you believe this?

A. Because the Sacred Scriptures plainly teach that the function of government was always implied as belonging only to those who received instructions upon it; and these were always described as official persons (Rom. xii. 8; 1 Tim. v. 20-22; 1 Pet. v. 3), and fitted by skill to guide the Church, which is not a qualification for membership.—1 Tim. iii. 45; Acts ii. 41.

Q. 161. What is implied in the judicatorial power of the Church represented by her bishops?

A. The power dogmatic, Cor. iv. 12; Acts xv. 2, 6: the power disciplinal, Matt. xvi. 19; xviii. 18; 1 Tim. v. 19: the power declaratory, Acts xx. 27; 2 Tim. ii. 2.

Q. 162. But these teachings can only have authority through a council representing the whole of the Church?

A. Just so. Bishops and presbyters should together sit in council, and deliver their judgment as that of the Church.

Q. 163. What is the system which our own Church provides?

A. Convocation.

Q. 164. Why?

A. Because the commission authoritatively to declare the mind of Christ respecting all the affairs, dogmatic and disciplinal, of His Church, was given not to members, but to the overseers and presbyters of the Church. When we say "The Church" enjoins, or orders, or agrees, we mean the authority which she has in the way of her synods and governors.

Q. 165. Is spiritual obedience and submission to pastors and spiritual rulers imposed upon the laity?

A. The Church authority has a threefold origin. The authority of the people, which is represented in the deacons, the Scripture authority represented in the priest, and the prophesying authority represented in the bishop. A single individual mind must have overwhelming reasons for convictions which run counter to an agreement of the majority of these, aiming at peace and truth. Plainly does Scripture enforce this teaching, as if foreseeing it would frequently be ignored, or denied, or set at defiance.

Q. 166. What is the meaning of the words, "Tell it unto the Church?"—Matt. xviii. 17.

A. The Church was the portion so called, as deciding with authority. The Church declares this, or demands that—is equivalent to the settled and conjoint opinion of bishops and presbyters, and others holding office of a spiritual nature; in fact, the judgment-seat of its official representatives and rulers is said to be that of the Church. In no other way could the "Church" be appealed to, especially at the period the words were used when the Church consisted of many thousands, and when the method of government was elementary, and altogether unsettled, as well as undefined. Our Lord did neither settle or define.

Q. 167. Is there any circumstantial evidence of this in the New Testament?

A. Yes. The excommunication of the incestuous person (1 Cor. v. 1-5; 2 Cor. ii. 6, 7) is described as a punishment inflicted by many: shewing the concurrent action of the church at Corinth was merged into the dictum of those who ruled and represented its individual opinions.

Q. 168. Did the various congregations and their spiritual pastors, in the towns of Jerusalem, Antioch, Ephesus, and Corinth, constitute separate churches?

A. Yes, separate churches; that is, the various congregations in Antioch, for instance, were united in the Church of Antioch, and so with the rest.

Q. 169. When the Synod of Jerusalem met, was their decision binding upon all the Churches?

A. Yes.

Q. 170. How was their decision arrived at?

A. By discussion, by consideration of facts, and by reference to the written Word.—Acts xv. 6-21.

Q. 171. Was this then not equivalent to the supposition that one chief Church had power over all?

A. Not according to ordinary and unbiassed reasoning, since the twelve apostles were representatives of, and stood in stead of, each and every individual Church that they had founded. It was a concourse of represented Churches, not solely the Church of Jerusalem, that in fact made up a general council. The Church of England would willingly have acknowledged the Churcʰ of Constantinople to be the chief of the Eastern world, as that of Rome was of the Western portion, *when all the world was ruled by the Roman Empire seated in authority at either capital.*

Q. 172. How, then, should a Church act with regard to districts, missions, and other important operations?

A. Rightly, the organization should be in the Church herself.

Q. 173. Is it so in the Church of England?

A. Unfortunately its connection with the State makes it necessary to resort to informal machinery.

Q. 174. What is convocation?

A. A body politic or ecclesiastical parliament, consisting of an upper and lower house. They were formed upon the model of early provincial synods, and date from a far earlier period than the Parliament of England.

Q. 175. Is there any authority over them?

A. Yes. By an Act called the Submission Act of Henry VIII., the royal writ must precede the assembling of convocation, as also the royal license before attempting or enacting canons.

Q. 176. Can bishops call synods without a license?

A. Yes; there is no law against their doing so, as, in fact, the sole authority to call a diocesan synod lies with them.

Q. 177. What is the difference between a synod, council, and general or œcumenical council?

A. It is difficult to draw a distinctive line: generally, a synod is an assembly of the bishop and his clergy in the diocese; council, a general assembly of bishops, and sometimes presbyters, and even laity, who removed when doctrinal subjects were to be discussed; œcumenic council, of nations. Synod is the Greek word for council, for Greece was the land of public assemblies.

Q. 178. Give a short account of convocation.

A. There is no doubt that in the second century there will be found models of an assembly in council, which we call convocation; and grievous scandals which the Church endures, and has no power to remove, began when synods ceased to sit. The tyrannical acts of Edward I. have led many to date the system of synodical action used in our Church to that period. The language of the Tulco Bishop of London in 1255, in the synod of London, declared that pope and king should not, though stronger than he, deprive him of his episcopal liberty, though they might take his mitre. In the time of Edward II., the king directed his writ to Archbishop Raynold to summon a provincial synod of Canterbury. The first instance of an absolute tone being used by the king in bidding a metropolitan to assemble his synod, occurred in the year 1290. In 1295, a clause was for the first time inserted in the bishop's writ to parliament, by which convocation of clergy was, as it were, assembled by royal writ into the presence of the king's lay deputies, with whom the members of the synod were to treat about a state subsidy for the Scottish war. The archbishop withdrew this mandate, and summoned in canonical way a convocation at St Paul's in 1314. A like course was pursued at York. This was the beginning of a milder, but still urgent course of supremacy over the ecclesiastical power. Ultimately, in the time of King Edward III., these rankling sores were healed by a commission between regal and metropolitanical authority in the formal method of assembling convocations, which obtains to this day (1327). The writ of

King Edward III. is, in fact, very similar to that of
Queen Victoria. Convocations were often held only
by metropolitan authority, without writ from the king.
The meetings of convocation were held at first at St
Paul's, afterwards at Westminster.

Q. 179. What was the general notion of convocation
from the period of Henry VIII.?

A. From 1530 (the famous year in which *Convocation*
granted the title of " supreme head, as far as the law of
Christ permits," to Henry VIII.), and thenceforward the
clergy were not directed to retire to debate on the
matter before convocation, for they were gradually becoming habituated to separate into two houses. Bishops,
abbots, and priors constituted the upper house. Sometimes bishops and metropolitan alone, distinct from
other clergy whatever. The office of prolocutor or
general president arose from this constitution of things,
as *organum cleri* to the upper house.

Q. 180. Did convocation have a penal power?

A. Yes. Occasionally, as in the case of John Wathe,
in 1424, who was condemned by Archbishop Chichely
to public punishment, riding on horseback without a
saddle, with the documents forged by him hung round
his neck. Usually the penal power was handed over to
the civil.

Q. 181. Was there any reduction in the number of the
members of convocation after the dissolution of religious
houses?

A. Yes. From 440 to 168, in the provincial synod
of Canterbury. In that of York, from 96 to 55. The
upper civil synod, that is the parliament, was diminished by nearly thirty members.

Q. 182. Did Queen Mary summon convocation?

A. Yes; and used the title, " Supreme Head of the Church of England."

Q. 183. Why was that convocation a pretended one ?

A. Because the Archbishop of Canterbury was in the Tower, and deprived from synodical action; and such influence used, so that none of King Edward's clergy were among the lower house. Robert Holgate, Archbishop of York, was also in prison.

Q. 184. In the pretended convocation, what celebrated disputation was appointed to take place on the 23rd of October ?—(Foxe's Acts and Min :).

A. The dispute on the doctrine of the Sacrament.

Q. 185. Was there another pretended synod ?

A. Yes, at Oxford in 1554, and was as pretended as the former, for the like reasons. A disputation ended in the martyrdom of Cranmer, Ridley, and Latimer. Rome here was as usual glad enough to countenance an unheard of proceeding, provided it was favourable to her views, namely, that an archbishop and two bishops should be tried for heresy by Royal commission.

Q. 186. What dastardly proceeding took place in November 1554 ?

A. The absolution given by Cardinal Pole to the Lords and Commons in Parliament on their knees.

Q. 187. Did they go thus far for no good reason ?

A. Yes. They received, in the statute restoring the Pope's authority, a clause securing the present possessors of all confiscated Church property.

Q. 188. When did Queen Mary die ?

A. On the 17th of November 1558, and Cardinal Pole a few hours afterwards.

Q. 189. Did a convocation meet immediately after Queen Elizabeth's accession ?

A. Yes, in 1559, N.S. Bonner being president.

Q. 190. Was this a real synod?

A. No; for they were Roman Catholic, and not English clergy who represented the Church assembled. The parliament met the day afterwards, and restored, as far as their authority went, matters connected with religion to the state in which they were left by Edward VI. The words " Supreme Head " were changed to Supreme Governor.

Q. 191. Did convocation, as some popular writers declare, have little to do with the services and articles, and general reformation?

A. It is an observation of writers utterly ignorant of, and opposed to the Church and its history. The synod did the work, though the State superintended, so that it was done in a legal and justifiable mode. The acts of synod, for instance, restored the cup to the laity, discharged clerical celibacy in 1547, made the first reformed Prayer-Book in 1548, the Ordinal of 1549, the two Reformed Prayer-Books 1552, and the Forty-Two Articles of 1552. Corroborative evidence is ample for this, and for more than this ; but ignorance of Church history, and learning in profane history, frequently go together.

Q. 192. Mention one of the most important synods which plainly was the voice of the Church in the sixteenth century, Elizabeth being queen?

A. That of 1563, which began the formation of the Thirty-Nine Articles, under Archbishop Parker.

Q. 193. Did they have the authority of both provinces?

A. Yes. Their title in Latin and English proves it.

Q. 194. State the words, than which nothing can be

wiser, more moderate, and more real, whereby, in the declaration preceding the Articles of 1562, the kingly power in Church matters is defined?

A. " That We are Supreme Governour of the Church of *England*: And that if any difference arise about the *external Policy*, concerning the *Injunctions*, *Canons*, and other *Constitutions* whatsoever thereto belonging, the Clergy in their Convocation is to order and settle them, having first obtained leave under our Broad Seal so to do: and We approving their said Ordinances and Constitutions; providing that none be made contrary to the Laws and Customs of the Land. That out of our Princely Care that the Churchmen may do the Work which is proper unto them, the Bishops and Clergy, from time to time in Convocation, upon their humble Desire, shall have Licence under our Broad Seal to deliberate of, and to do all such Things, as, being made plain by them, and assented unto by Us, shall concern the settled Continuance of the Doctrine and Discipline of the Church of *England* now established; from which We will not endure any varying or departing in the least Degree."

Q. 195. What does this assert?

A. That the king is supreme governor of the Church of England. That the external policy is to be considered and settled by convocation, as well as the internal arrangements of the Church. That the king so far interferes as protector and asserter of the rights of the Church to be supported by the law in what she promulgates and teaches. A record of convocation in 1604 also refers to the fact.

Q. 196. But is there not some doubt about a portion of the synod?

A. Yes. It is difficult to know in what manner the lower house of the York Province testified their consent. But as nothing has been said against it, it is beyond all ordinary discussion.

Q. 197. Do they differ from the Articles of 1552-3?

A. Yes. They were reduced from forty-two to thirty-nine, and some trifling alterations were made.

Q. 198. Did any work of instruction, fitted for the people, receive authority?

A. Yes. Dean Nowell's Catechism.

Q. 199. What remarkable popular effort was made?

A. A schedule signed by thirty-three members of the lower house, urged very foolish innovations, amongst the rest, the removal of organs as a grievance to conscience!

Q. 200. By the Canons of 1603, what is stated to be the Church of England by representation?

A. The convocation of Canterbury and York, when assembled in the name of Christ and by the Queen's authority.

Q. 201. Is it to be desired that convocation and diocesan synods should be restored to working order?

A. Most desirable; and it is to be hoped that ere long the people will see the necessity of calling God's blessing upon such solemn acts of mutual consideration and discussion as they involve, and by which alone peace and restoration of discipline and good order can alone be enforced.

PART VI.

CHAPTER VI.

ECONOMY OF THE CHURCH.

Q. 202. What is patronage of the laity?

A. It is a legal right to present to a living, with or without the cure of souls, acquired by purchase or by inheritance.

Q. 203. Is this not Simony, when a cleric presents himself?

A. Not legally. The sin of Simon Magus was to obtain to himself spiritual authority and gifts (Acts viii. 18): a rightly ordained clergyman has this.

Q. 204. Is it nevertheless objectionable, even legally, to buy and sell livings and the cure of souls?

A. Doubtless it is, and open to much evil; it is secularizing the privilege of choosing or nominating a priest to a cure.

Q. 205. If the people invite and call, would that be likely to work better?

A. No. It is, in fact, secularizing the privilege as much as giving it to a lay patron, only differing, in being worse that a mob should rule in divine things.

Q. 206. What is the right and scriptural way?

A. That the people search for a right person among themselves, and that he should be subject, previous to ordination by the bishop, to remonstrance and objection on the part of the laity assembled in church.

Q. 207. Is that the apostolical method?

A. It is very analogous. As nearly as the altered circumstances of things allow, it is the system adopted by the Church of England, in commanding a document (called from the two first words in Latin a " Si quis," a kind of challenge) to be publicly read by the officiating clergyman at Morning Service in the parish Church of the candidate for orders, in order that any one objecting to his ordination may communicate with the bishop, who will find means to ascertain the facts stated.

Q. 208. What is the authority of the " Canons " of 1603, in time of James I.

A. As enacted by the clergy, and not confirmed by parliament, they are not binding on the laity at least, and in so far as not ancient canon law, need not much of the regard of the clergy. But they shew in what spirit the Church reformed herself at the time of the suppression of Papal intrusion. The authority of the old canon law of England, saving and except where the statute law modifies it (as the Pragmatic Code restrains it in France), should be binding upon all men. The canons are obligatory when agreeing with ancient canon law.

Q. 209. What is the jurisdiction of the parish priest ?

A. The parochial territory, originally assigned by bishops, is the rectorial sphere of authority in governing the people and administering the sacraments. He has no external powers, not even that of excommunication, without information and priority of the bishop.

Q. 210. In what is the power of the bishop ?

A. In him is the plenitude of the priesthood, power, orders, and jurisdiction. He has power of external government of the Church as a body, and of the internal government of souls—in fine, he possesses the power of bishop and priest.

Q. 211. Is there any precedent for the assumed superiority of the Bishop of Rome?

A. None. The idea only arose from the accident of the Roman Empire having dominion over the civilized world. Would Rome confess it, we are all in union one with another, at least all bishops of the Universal Church. To be in subjection to the Roman bishop is in fact the true and sole desire of Rome, not "union."

Q. 212. Is a bishop subject to any other higher power?

A. Yes, to the Church in synod assembled, which has ever declared the faith, and regulated from time to time the discipline of the body Catholic. "Paul, or Apollos, or Cephas; all are yours." This at once destroys all Papal assumption, as it also does away with all mere Episcopalianism; for bishops have from all time been subject to the canons.

Q. 213. What is the means of support for the clergy?

A. The property of the Church. The inequality of incomes is on the whole useful, and even necessary; for if they were all divided equally between bishops, deans, the scholastic, governing, and working clergy, it would appear that £150 per annum is the most each would receive.

Q. 214. How is the fabric of the Church supported?

A. It ought to be supported by all; but perhaps, under the necessities of the age, Dissenters should be relieved on demand and signification of their schism.

Q. 215. Whose duty is it to take the oversight of this, and other minor matters connected with the services?

A. That of the church wardens (anciently called the ecclesiæ guardiani), as representatives of the body of parishioners.

Q. 216. Give some account of them?

A. They are lay officers, chosen respectively (but not always) by the parson and parish. They in theory, are those who look to the behaviour of the parishioners, and present offenders to the ecclesiastical courts. Dissenters can by deputy, but irregularly they in person discharge the office. Organs, bells, surplices, &c., are their property, as vested with them in the name of the parish.

Q. 217. Can it be supposed that Church endowments were originally intended, without any exception, for the benefit of Dissenters as well as Church people, and to be subject to the distribution of a parliamentary committee?

A. It is the object of Dissenters to act upon this idea, although in direct opposition to all legal right, and to the ancient rights of Church endowments, dating from the sixth to the nineteenth century; besides, the Church is an institution older than the monarchy, and not always a part of the public interest, since the public were, in some part, heathens when it existed.

Q. 218. How do you explain this?

A. The Christian Church existed during the Saxon Witenagemot, and in Wales when there were but chieftains and serfs. The Church then was a distinct institution, not proceeding from, or of the State, although for the benefit of all in it.

Q. 219. Is it not liable to the contingencies of legislation, as connected with a State Church?

A. Yes, as far as property can be dealt with, which is as much that of the Church as a man's estate is his own.

Q. 220. What are tithes?

A. Tithes were first legally enjoined by Moses—Lev. xxvii. 30. The tithe given by Abraham to Melchizedek was a free and voluntary gift from the spoils, not from the possessions of Abraham; probably as a priestly homage. The Levites gave a tenth of their tithe to the priests. They were ceremonial in the law, for (Num. xviii. 24, 28) they were not given to the Levites till they had been first offered as an heave-offering to the Lord.

Q. 221. When do we first hear of them in the Christian Church?

A. In a provincial synod at Cullen in 356.

Q. 222. When were they first introduced into this country?

A. In 794, by Offa, King of Mercia, to atone for his murdering Ethelbert, King of East Angles. They first became, by the law of Offa, property and inheritance by way of land.

Q. 223. Was a tithe-gift common by tradition even among heathens?

A. Yes. The Romans gave a tenth of the spoils taken in war to Jupiter, hence called Prædator.

Q. 224. Did St Augustine receive tithes?

A. Yes, by way of gift in land from the King of Kent, and donations from private individuals. Gregory the Great ordered the tithes to be divided into four parts—one of the parts being for the poor and another for repair and erection of churches. This was, in fact, the old law of the Church.

Q. 225. Has the law of tithes remained much the same since the time of Henry the Eighth?

A. Practically it has, although much altered.

Q. 226. He confiscated church property, did he not?

D

A. Yes; every kind of sacred property.

Q. 227. Did not Henry VIII. do in fact what the Dissenters desire to do now, if they could?

A. No. All he did was, to do without a concordat what France had in effect done with it. He abolished the supremacy of the Pope, which had existed only in semblance frequently, and was oftentimes ignored; he suppressed monasteries, which had been done before, and was done after, by Roman Princes and Popes; and reformed certain practical abuses. Purification of faith and ritual was not introduced till the times of Edward VI. and Elizabeth. And although the way all this was effected, and the misery it caused to many holy men and women, is much to be deplored, yet the general profligacy of the monastic order was an undeniable fact.

Q. 228. What represented, in the Ante-Reformed Church, the dissenting interest of modern days?

A. The religious houses and bodies of wandering friars, who were exempted from Episcopal authority, and only under the Pope. Grostete, Bishop of Lincoln, visited the houses in 1237, in defiance of these irregular privileges, and compelled them to live according to rule.

Q. 229. Was the Reformation, at least its elementary character in the time of Henry VIII., an innovation on ritual or faith of antecedent periods?

A. No; rather a return to former purity: the Church was still presided over by a Gardiner, a cathedral by its dean and canons, instead of prior and monks—which was restoring the ancient constitution; high mass, and doctrines undisputed by Rome were preached; there was, in fact, but one religious community in the country for many years after Reform had commenced.

Q. 230. Did the country act as if it changed its idea of the legal continuity of the Church and its constitutions?

A. No; it was a society changed as in opinions and practices, but legally the same. It was a garden cleared, and swept, and replanted, but the same nevertheless.

Q. 231. The clergy and laity acknowledged, and afterwards ignored the Pope's authority; and bishops remained in their dioceses under all the varied conditions of the Church?

A. Yes; Pole succeeded Cranmer; Parker regularly succeeded Pole; and Kitchen, Bishop of Cardiff, remained through all the variations.

Q. 232. Did any confiscation take place?

A. Yes; confiscation of endowments specially given in masses for the dead, and the maintenance of chantries.

Q. 233. There is no legal or historical proof of Church property being the property of the people?

A. None whatever; the state can have no more power of that than over any other personal and private property, which is, and must be, subject to legal control. Otherwise, the endowment of a bishop, or Church, or Cathedral, would be a mere application of taxes to pay a public servant, or army, or office; no benefactor ever supposed alienation and confiscation or appropriation of his offerings to serve various sectaries.

Q. 234. Can they have a right to Church ordinances who refuse to share the responsibility its communion gives?

A. Absolutely none, beyond that which violence and might may extort.

Q. 235. Is not this uncharitable and intolerant?

A. No. The Christian religion is absolutely intolerant in the sense of the words of our Saviour,—" He that gathereth not with me, scattereth." It admits of one God, one Lord, one baptism, one faith, alone, and for ever. Men will not be saved by what they " dissent" from the Church, but by what they consent to. Calvin, Knox, Brown, Wesley, Whitefield, etc, could not so interpret Sacred Scripture as to avoid the application to them of the above words, for they could not, nor could any one, so interpret Sacred Scripture as to unite around their individual will-worship the amount of authority, erudition, and spiritual influence which the Church has, otherwise they must assume infallibility.

Q. 236. Is the Church infallible?

A. Yes, as far as the truth as it is in Jesus is upheld, for she is the pillar and ground of the truth. The " Bible" contains infallible means of salvation. What the Bible is has been decided by the Church, and in that sense she holds the infallible position. In that sense the Pope is infallible, and in no other.

Q. 237. Explain further.

A. If persons were to write down what truths were undoubted—and whether in these truths all men believing would be infallible; then, if the Church holds such, her belief is infallible, and she is so far infallible.

Q. 238. Who are its members here on earth?

A. We have criteria to mark them: who will be in the Church Invisible will be seen in the great day only.

DOCTRINAL QUESTIONS,

WITH ANSWERS CHIEFLY FOUNDED UPON THE PRAYER
BOOK, THE THIRTY-NINE ARTICLES, AND
THE CATECHISM.

Q. 1. What is the meaning of trinity in unity, and unity in trinity?

A. That there is but one living and true God, everlasting, without body, parts, or passions, "and in unity of this Godhead there be three Persons, of one substance, power, and eternity; the Father, the Son, and the Holy Ghost."—Art. i.

Q. 2. What does the word "mystery" mean?

A. That which is not explicable according to the usual experience of humanity.

Q. 3. Was God the Holy Ghost present at the creation?

A. Yes. The Spirit of God moved upon the face of the waters.—Gen. i. 2.

Q. 4. Was the Sabbath instituted before the law of Moses distinguished that institution by special command?

A. Yes. "On the seventh day God ended His work," and blessed the seventh day and sanctified it.—Gen. ii. 2.

Q. 5. What is meant by the fall?

A. The sin of disobedience in Adam transgressing God's command not to touch the forbidden fruits.

Q. 6. How did that influence man?

A. It made his nature prone and inclining to evil,

whereby man is very far gone from original righteousness, and is of his own nature inclined to evil.—Art. ix.

Q. 7. Does this inclination to sin remain after baptism?

A. Yes. And this infection of nature doth remain, yea in them that are regenerated; whereby the lust of the flesh is not subject to the law of God. And although there is no condemnation for them that believe and are baptized, yet the Apostle doth confess, that concupiscence and lust hath of itself the nature of sin.—Art. ix.

Q. 8. Does regeneration take place in baptism?

A. Yes, we are regenerated or converted then once for all.

Q. 9. Prove it?

A. In the baptismal service, after the rite, the priest says,—Seeing, brethren, that this child is regenerate, and grafted into the body of Christ's Church, let us give thanks unto Almighty God for these benefits; and with one accord make our prayers unto Him, that this child may lead the rest of his life according to this beginning. The 27th Article says,—It is also a sign of regeneration or new birth, whereby, as by an instrument, they that receive baptism rightly are grafted into the Church; the promises of the forgivenness of sin, and of our adoption to be the sons of God by the Holy Ghost, are visibly signed and sealed; faith is confirmed and grace increased by virtue of prayer unto God.

Q. 10. What do those, who say this is not the doctrine of the Church, advance?

A. They mistake their own views for those of the Church, in not distinguishing between regeneration and such a change as occurs in the wicked who suddenly are renewed to a righteous life.

Q. 11. What does our Church say of deadly sin after baptism ?

A. " After we have received the Holy Ghost, we may depart from grace given, and fall into sin, and by the grace of God we may arise again and amend our lives."—Art. xvi.

Q. 12. Are there any who desire to alter this ?

A. Yes, all Puritans and Dissenters.

Q. 13. What do you mean by "Incarnation ?"

A. That Christ took our nature upon Him, not by conversion of the Godhead into flesh, " but by taking of the manhood into God."—Athan. Cr.

Q. 14. What is sanctification ?

A. Grace to withstand the temptations of the world, the flesh, and the devil, and with pure hearts and minds to follow Thee the only God.—Collect for 18th Sunday after Trinity.

Q. 15. What does this teach as to the doctrine ?

A. That sanctification is gradual and continual.

Q. 16. May it be a sudden change ?

A. It may be, but it is not ordinarily the way the Holy Ghost acts.

Q. 17. Is there any text to shew that the Church is divine, though ministered to and served by men ?

A. Yes, 1 Tim. iii. 5 and 15, where St Paul, delaying his coming, and placing Timothy over the Church, writes that he may know how to behave himself in the house of God—which is the Church of God, the pillar and ground of the truth.

Q. 18. What is the visible Church ?

A. The visible Church of Christ is a congregation of faithful men, in the which the pure word of God is preached, and the sacraments be duly minister according to Christ's ordinance in all those things that of necessity are requisite to the same.—Art. xix.

Q. 19. Does this correspond with Sacred Scripture ?

A. Yes. See Acts ii. 42.

Q. 20. What are those "things" requisite to due administration of sacraments, according to Church ordinances ?

A. Apostolic succession of authority, which the Church of England has by three ways—the ancient Irish, British, and Roman.

Q. 21. What does our Church say with regard to her desire to restore "penance" for sin, and wicked life and conversation, in her lapsed members ?

A. She says in her Communion Service : Brethren, in the Primitive Church there was a godly discipline, that, at the beginning of Lent, such persons as stood convicted of notorious sin were put to open penance, and punished in this world, that their souls might be saved in the day of the Lord; and that others, admonished by their example, might be the more afraid to offend. Instead whereof (until the said discipline may be restored again, which is much to be wished), it is thought good, that at this time (in the presence of you all) should be read the general sentences of God's cursing against impenitent sinners.

Q. 22. What is the doctrine of our Church as to Holy Scripture ?

A. Holy Scripture containeth all things necessary to salvation ; so that whatsoever is not read therein, nor may be proved thereby, is not to be required of any man, that it should be believed as an article of the faith, or be thought requisite or necessary to salvation.

Q. 23. Why is the Apocrypha read ?

A. For example of life and instruction of manners; but yet doth it not apply them to establish any doctrine.

Q. 24. When were the apocryphal writings received by a part of the Church?

A. At the Council of Trent.

Q. 25. In what words does our church admit, but limit private judgment?

A. In the Collect for Whitsunday, the Almighty is besought, in the Holy Ghost, to teach that judgment, and to grant us by the same Spirit to have a right judgment in all things, and evermore to rejoice in His holy comfort.

Q. 26. What does our Church state as to "reading" of Holy Scriptures? Does "reading," in her judgment, supersede the necessity of her teaching and light?

A. No; but that we may hear them, read, mark, learn, and inwardly digest them.

Q. 27. Does she not enjoin reading Sacred Scripture with a view to those objects? or does she mention that rites, ceremonies, and controverted points are to be gathered out of the Bible, as an independent authority, sufficient for any individual, to oppose her teaching?

A. No. She desires, with wise foresight, her members so to read, that by patience, and comfort of God's holy Word, they may embrace, and ever hold fast the blessed hope of everlasting life, which is given them in Christ Jesus. But many use their liberty for a cloak of maliciousness.

Q. 28. What is her only weapon against offenders?

A. She has none but what she should rightly have—the power of excommunication.—Rom. xvi. 17. In the 33rd Article she says,—That person which, by open denunciation of the Church, is rightly cut off from the unity of the Church, and excommunicated, ought to be taken of the whole multitude of the faithful, as an heathen and publican, until he be openly reconciled by penance, and received into the Church by a judge that hath authority thereunto.

Q. 29. What is the authority of the Church?

A. The Church hath power to decree rites or ceremonies, and authority in controversies of faith; and yet it is not lawful for the Church to ordain any thing that is contrary to God's Word written, neither may it so expound one place of Scripture, that it be repugnant to another.

Q. 30. As the Church recognizes the authority of the Four General Councils, how does she limit her requiring credibility to any, from her members?

A. According to the 21st Article, things ordained by them as necessary to salvation have neither strength nor authority, unless it may be declared that they be taken out of Holy Scripture.

Q. 31. Is this perhaps rather too strict?

A. Strict or not, it is her view; and with it her members must agree, or leave her communion.

Q. 32. What is the Church's voice upon keeping saints' days?

A. She keeps these sacred (marking them by using the holy communion service), which have ever been kept holy by the early Church, nor has she taken upon herself to add to them or to take from them. She prays, in the Collect for All Saints, that God, "who hast knit together Thine elect in one communion and fellowship, in the mystical body of Thy Son Christ our Lord, may grant us grace so to follow Thy blessed saints in all virtuous and godly living, that we may come to those unspeakable joys which Thou hast prepared for them that

unfeignedly love Thee, through Jesus Christ our Lord."
The saints are mentioned as God's—not those made of
the Church.

Q. 33. Is this according to Sacred Scripture?

A. Yes.—Heb. vi. 12. That ye be not slothful, but
followers of them who through faith and patience inherit
the promises.

Q. 34. How does she pray for unity; and in what
measure does she consider it to exist?

A. Such unity as is consistent with Christian belief,
and that which she allows in her communion, that the
whole body of the Church, "built upon the foundation
of the Apostles and Prophets, Jesus Christ himself being
the head corner-stone, may be so joined together in
unity of spirit by their doctrine, that we may be made
an holy temple acceptable unto thee; through Jesus
Christ our Lord."

Q. 35. Does she regard unity in worship and in rites
as obligatory upon every branch of her planting?

A. No; nor does she consider foreign churches under
any obligation to rules which are foreign to them. In
the preface to the Liturgy:—"And in these our doings
we condemn no other nations, nor prescribe any thing
but to our own people only; for we think it convenient
that every country should use such ceremonies as they
shall think best to the setting forth of God's honour and
glory, and to the reducing of the people to a most perfect and godly living, without error or superstition."

Q. 36. What creeds do we receive?

A. The creeds of the Universal Church.

Q. 37. Why are creeds necessary?

A. Because heresies and divisions continually increase. Even so early as St Paul's time, a profession

of uniformity was necessary. 1. Abstinence from pollution of idolatry. 2. From fornication. 3. From things strangled. 4. From blood. Besides, St John's Gospel was composed especially after heresy was spread abroad. So the creeds were written as systematic instruction necessary for the evil times.

Q. 38. Does Christianity need creeds?

A. No; but error needs to be met by "a form of sound words."

Q. 39. Supposing, for the sake of argument, Episcopal Apostolic succession not to be an indispensable mark of a church, how would that affect the Church?

A. It would affect a mere community of Christians outside the Church; for at most, it is no harm or drawback to the integrity of Christianity or Christian life. On the other hand, to all sects, from Presbyterianism downwards, if it be, as all antiquity agree, a *sine qua non* for valid administration of the Eucharist and other rites, they who have it not are *unsafe*, even in the mildest view.

Q. 40. What is the difference between the ancient Catholic faith and Roman innovations, and compare the moderation of the Church of England?

Papistry.	The Catholic Church and Church of England.
A. 1. The spiritual and temporal autocracy of the Pope.	Superior rank of Bishop of Rome may be allowed in her communion.
2. Compulsory celibacy of priesthood.	Not existing in the Primitive Church, or in the Greek or English.
3. Solitary mass.	Not known in the Church till the 4th century.

4. Denial of the chalice.	Arose about the thirteenth century, and therefore denied to be the teaching of the church.
5. Transubstantiation.	Introduced in the year 831 by Paschatus Radbertus.
6. Compulsory auricular confession.	Introduced by Pope Leo in 448, therefore denied by the Church.
7. Mariolatry. 8. Hagiolatry.	First arose in a daily office instituted in 1050; in 1136 the canons of Lyons introduced the doctrine in the offices, and were opposed by St Bernard.
9. Purgatory.	Scarcely known till Gregory the Great, expressly limiting it to venial sin, promulgated the doctrine: therefore not known to the early Church.
10. Supererogatory merits.	Indulgence, as far as relaxation in ecclesiastical punishment, not denied. In present form first introduced in the 11th century.
11. Limitation of Catholic Church to one Episcopal.	From the time of Hildebrand, and Council of 1059, not even discussed in any shape till the 9th century.

Q. 41. Can you mention any text to shew what believing in Christ means?

A. It involves the statements of the Creeds.

1 St John iv. 15.—Whosoever shall confess that Jesus is the Son of God.

—— v. 5.—Who is he that overcometh the world, but he that believeth that Jesus is the Son of God.

——, v. 1.—Whosoever believeth that Jesus is the Christ.

—— v. 13.—You that believe on the name of the Son of God.

Q. 42. How are the three Creeds one?

A. In the same sense that the four Gospels are one.

Q. 43. Does the Church of England charitably include all Christian communities in the Church Catholic?

A. In so far as they hold doctrines or portions of faith, she holds so far they are of the Catholic Church. —Collects for Good Friday. Just as our Lord told the Samaritan woman, salvation was of the Jews : yet Judah He much loved, though His name was also great in Israel.

Q. 44. What does our Church say of the necessity of the three orders?

A. In the preface to her Service for ordaining priests and deacons, she saith,—It is evident unto all men diligently reading the Holy Scripture and ancient authors, that from the Apostles' time there have been three orders of ministers in Christ's Church : bishops, priests, and deacons; which offices were evermore had in such reverend estimation, that no man might presume to execute any of them, except they were first called, tried, examined, and known to have such qualities as are requisite for the same; and also by publick prayer, with imposition of hands, were approved and admitted thereunto by lawful authority.

Q. 45. Does not the rubric prefixed to the Baptism Service state that baptism must be given by a lawful minister; and if so, what is a lawful minister?

A. Yes. "First, let the minister of the parish (or, in his absence, any other *lawful minister* that can be procured)," &c., &c. "No man shall be accounted or taken to be a lawful bishop, priest, or deacon in the United Church of England and Ireland, or suffered to execute any of the said functions, except he be called, tried, examined, and admitted thereunto, according to the form hereafter following, or hath had formerly episcopal consecration or ordination."—Rubric to Service for ordering of Deacons.

Q. 46. What do many Dissenters and false Church people say baptism is?

A. Just what the 27th Article says it is not—a "sign of profession," a mere "mark of difference."

Q. 47. Does the Church consider religion and its forms a matter of mere agreement and choice between God and his created beings?

A. No. In the 18th Article she saith,—They also are to be had accursed that presume to say, that every man shall be saved by the law or sect which he professeth, so that he be diligent to frame his life according to that law and the light of nature.

Q. 48. What are the primary means of grace, and what the secondary?

A. 1. The sacraments.

2. Prayer, fasting, and reading God's Word.

3. Instruction—"faith cometh by hearing, and hearing by the word of God."

Q. 49. Why does our Church command us to kneel at the Lord's Supper?

A. "Kneeling is well meant for a signification of our humble and grateful acknowledgment of the benefits of Christ therein given to all worthy receivers, and for the avoiding of such profanation and disorder in the holy communion, as might otherwise ensue."—Rubric at end of Communion Service.

Q. 50. Where is the natural body of our Saviour Christ?

A. "The natural body and blood of our Saviour Christ are in heaven, and not here; it being against the truth of Christ's natural body to be at one time in more places than one."—Rubric at end of Communion Service.

Q. 51. Are the elements "holy" after consecration?

A. Yes. Unspeakably holy, sacred, and separated, so that after consecration, the priest is to return to the Lord's table, and reverently place upon it what remaineth of the consecrated elements, covering the same with a fair linen cloth.—Rubric.

Q. 52. How is the "real presence" acknowledged by our Church?

A. By her writers and defenders generally after such manner as obtained in the early Church. In her voice, as by her Prayer Book, she refrains from explanations. For as grace in baptism is not changed into the water, or the water into it, so she says with the Apostle—my body—the communion of my body; my blood—the communion of my blood. Better be dumb than rashly to define that inscrutable presence, subjected to our faith, but not revealed to our understanding, or rather for the understanding of which no power has been vouchsafed to us in this life.

Q. 53. What does the Holy Eucharist become to the unworthy ?

A. It hardens them, just as the sun is the same "presence," either hardening as on clay, or melting as on wax.

Q. 54. What does the Church chiefly look to?

A. The act to be done, and not to be discussed: that whatever may be the nature of the real presence, we try "so to eat the flesh of thy dear Son Jesus Christ, and to drink his blood, that our sinful bodies may be made clean by his body, and our souls washed through his most precious blood, and that we may evermore dwell in him, and he in us."

Q. 55. What does the Catechism teach ?

A. That the body and blood of Christ are verily and indeed taken and received by the faithful in the Lord's Supper.

Q. 56. Can you explain this, touching the point of wicked receivers ?

A. Yes ; in the prayer after reception—the true receiver, the faithful, are those " who have duly received the holy mysteries."

Q. 57. What is the nature of the " sacrifice" we offer, and what do we shew forth ?

A. We desire, in the prayer after reception, our Heavenly Father mercifully to accept this our sacrifice of praise and thanksgiving.—See 1 Cor. xi. 26.

Q. 58. Is there any adoration offered ?

A. None to any corporal presence of Christ's natural flesh and blood.

Q. 59. In what way do we adore ? .

E

A. With a true penitent heart and lively faith we receive the Holy Sacrament, by which we spiritually eat the flesh of Christ, and drink his blood; then we dwell in Christ, and Christ in us; we are one with Christ, and Christ with us.

Q. 60. What does our Church teach further?

A. Right or wrong, it is our duty to believe her teaching, which certainly declares, that the reception of the body and blood of Christ does not depend upon the absolute reception of the elements, thereby crushing at once transubstantiation or consubstantiation, or any definition of mode of presence whatever.

Q. 61. How do you prove this?

A. From the words of rubric in Communion of the Sick. "But if a man, either by reason of extremity of sickness, or for want of warning in due time to the curate, or for lack of company to receive with him, or by any other just impediment, do not receive the Sacrament of Christ's body and blood, the curate shall instruct him, that if he do truly repent him of his sins, and steadfastly believe that Jesus Christ hath suffered death upon the cross for him, and shed his blood for his redemption, earnestly remembering the benefits he hath thereby, and giving him hearty thanks therefore, he doth eat and drink the body and blood of our Saviour Christ profitably to his soul's health, although he do not receive the sacrament with his mouth.

Q. 62. What text, in connection with the celebration of the Holy Eucharist, shews the necessity of preparation?

A. 1 Cor. xi. 31. If we would judge ourselves, we should not be judged.

Q. 63. When we celebrate the Holy Eucharist, what do we shew forth?

A. The Lord's death till he come.—1 Cor. xi. 26.

Q. 64. What is " faith ;" and define " repentance?

A. Repentance, whereby we forsake sin ; and faith, whereby we steadfastly believe the promises of God.

Q. 65. Why do we command infants to be baptised, who cannot have both or either?

A. Because they promise them both by their sureties.

Q. 66. When and by what are we justified ; and what does the word signify?

A. In baptism, and by " faith only."—Art. xi. " We are accounted righteous before God by faith only."

Q. 67. What are the significant words used in reference to baptism in the 16th Article?

A. " Not every deadly sin willingly committed after baptism is sin against the Holy Ghost—thereby signifying, that the Holy Ghost is given in baptism."

Q. 68. When are works " good ?"

A. Only after justification, as in the 12th Article ; for good works, which are the fruits of faith, and follow after justification, cannot put away our sins, and endure the severity of God's judgment.

Q. 69. What do you mean by a " state of salvation?"

A. The condition of being a member of Christ, the child of God, and an inheritor of the kingdom of heaven.

Q. 70. What proof is there that the doctrine of baptismal regeneration, held by our Church, does not mean what is called " the great change," or " conversion," by Dissenters, and those ministers in the Church of England holding similar views with Dissenters ?

A. The words of the prayer : " Almighty and ever-living God, who hast vouchsafed to regenerate these thy servants by water and the Holy Ghost, and hast given unto them forgiveness of all their sins."

Q. 71. What does this shew?

A. That if ministers do not believe this, they do not believe what is taught by the Church, and which was sworn to be taught at the reception of orders.

Q. 72. What is confirmation?

A. A rite in which persons, who have learned " what their godfathers and godmothers promised for them, may themselves, with their own mouth and consent, openly before the Church, ratify and confirm the same; and also promise, that by the grace of God they will evermore endeavour themselves faithfully to observe such things, as they, by their own confession, have assented unto."

Q. 73. Who instituted this rite?

A. The early Church by the apostles, as we learn in the 8th chapter of Acts.

Q. 74. Why is confirmation not a sacrament?

A. Because it wants one of the four marks mentioned in the Catechism, which are, 1. the outward and visible sign; 2. an inward and spiritual grace given unto us; 3. ordained by Christ himself, as a means whereby we receive the same; 4. a pledge to assure us of that grace given to us. The third mark is that which is wanted to complete this rite as a sacrament.

Q. 75. In what words is the inward grace mentioned by our Church; and what is the outward sign of confirmation?

A. 1. Strengthen them, we beseech Thee, O Lord, with the Holy Ghost the Comforter, and increase in them Thy manifold gifts of grace.

2. Laying on of the hands of the bishop.

Q. 76. What is our Church's doctrine of the soul's condition after death ?

A. It is sufficiently perceived what the mind of the Church is from the prayer in the Burial Service, in which she states her belief, that with God do live the spirits of them that depart hence in the Lord, and with whom the souls of the faithful, after they are delivered from the burden of the flesh, are in joy and felicity.

Q. 77. What is the doctrine of angels and their intercourse with the Church visible ?

A. In the Collect for St Michael's Day, she professes her belief that God has ordained and constituted the services of angels and men in a wonderful order ; and prays, " that as they do service in heaven, so by Thy appointment they may succour and defend us on earth, through Jesus Christ our Lord."

Q. 78. What is predestination ? and what is its reasonable proof of existence ?

A. A gift of God, by which they who have been " endued with so excellent a benefit of God, be called according to God's purpose by his Spirit working in due season: they through grace obey the calling. Those who feel in themselves the working of the Spirit of Christ, mortifying the works of the flesh, and their earthly members, and drawing up their mind to high and heavenly things, may rest assured of the presence of grace."—Art. xvii.

Q. 79. In what sense is " a new heart" used by our Church ?

A. The word is used in the Collect for Ash Wednesday to signify " that we, worthily lamenting our sins, and acknowledging our wretchedness, may obtain of Thee, the God of all mercy, perfect remission and forgiveness, through Jesus Christ our Lord."

Q. 80. How does our Church speak of fasting?

A. She enjoins, but does not command upon pain of displeasure, and leaves to each, as our Saviour did to His disciples, a choice of higher or inferior holiness, when He said that they failed in curing one difficult case of defilement, " because that kind came out by praying and fasting." She prays for "grace" to grant the right mind of fasting—in the Collect for first Sunday in Lent—" Give us grace to use such abstinence, that, our flesh being subdued to the Spirit, we may ever obey Thy godly motions in righteousness and true holiness, to Thy honour and glory."

Q. 81. Explain the following portions of the Lord's prayer.

A. 1. " Thy kingdom come."

1. " To send His grace unto me, and to all people."

2. " Thy will be done on earth as it is in heaven."

2. " That we may worship Him, serve Him, and obey Him, as we ought to do."

3. " Give us this day our daily bread."

3. " Pray unto God, that He will send us all things that be needful both for our souls and bodies."

4. " Lead us not into temptation."

4. " That it will please Him to save and defend us in all dangers, ghostly and bodily."

5. " But deliver us from evil."

5. "All sin and wickedness, from our ghostly enemy, and from everlasting death."

Q. 82. When does the Church begin her year?

A. At Advent; about the time when the world's year is drawing to its close. The seasons or periods of the Christian year are marked according to the birth, life, death, and doctrine of the Lord the Saviour—as Advent, Christmas, Epiphany, Three Sundays before Lent, Lent, Easter, Whitsuntide, and Sundays after Trinity Sunday.

Q. 83. What does the word "prevent" usually mean in the Liturgy?

A. It means "go before and lead," as in the Collect: We humbly beseech Thee, that, as by Thy special grace preventing us, Thou dost put into our minds good desires, so by Thy continual help we may bring the same to good effect.

Q. 84. What do the words, " O Lord, deal not with us after our sins," mean?

A. The word "after," signifies "according to."

Q. 85. What do the words, "kindly fruits of the earth," mean?

A. Kindly, "various kinds."

Q. 86. What do the words, "wealth," "wealthy," "with my body I Thee worship," mean?

A. Prosperity, power—do homage or endow.

Q. 87. What is meant by " Advent," Epiphany, Septuagesima, Ash-Wednesday, Lent, Easter, Rogation Days, Whitsuntide, Ember Day?

A. 1. Advent means " Coming."

2. Epiphany,—" Manifestation," derived from a Greek word. ·

3. Septuagesima, Sexagesima, Quinquagesima,— The 70th, 60th, 50th, days nearly before Easter Day.

4. Ash Wednesday,—The first day of Lent. In the early Church grievous sinners who were suspended from Church communion were restored after a course of penitence. They presented themselves for communion at the Church-door on the first day of Lent, covered or sprinkled with ashes or dust.

6. Easter,—" Rising."

7. Rogation,—meaning Supplication Days. The first three days of the week before Holy Thursday. They took their rise in the eighth century.

8. Whitsuntide,—the commemoration of the Descent of the fiery tongues. The early Church, considering that by outward signs or emblems much help was given to the people before printing, and the general use of the Scriptures, ordered the newly baptized to appear in white garments on this day.

9. Ember Days,—the periods at the four seasons when those chosen by the Laity for the service of the Church are ordained. The Wednesday, Friday, and Saturday preceding the Sunday of ordination are Ember Days. Ember is a Saxon word, signifying " rotation " or " course."

Q. 88. How many services has our Church?

A. She has services for her members to sanctify every

condition and duty of life, from birth to death. Daily Services, Communion and Litany Services, Services for Marriage, Baptism, Confirmation, Sickness, and Death. For ordaining Priests and Deacons, and consecrating Bishops, and other additional services.

A CATECHISM,

THAT IS TO SAY,

AN INSTRUCTION TO BE LEARNED OF EVERY PERSON, BEFORE HE BE BROUGHT TO BE CONFIRMED BY THE BISHOP.

Q. What is your name?

A. N. or M.

Q. Who gave you this name?

A. My Godfathers and Godmothers in my baptism; wherein I was made a member of Christ, the child of God, and an inheritor of the kingdom of heaven.

Q. What did your Godfathers and Godmothers then for you?

A. They did promise and vow three things in my name. First, that I should renounce the devil and all his works, the pomps and vanity of this wicked world, and all the sinful lusts of the flesh. Secondly, that I should believe all the Articles of the Christian Faith. And thirdly, that I should keep God's holy will and commandments, and walk in the same all the days of my life.

Q. Dost thou not think that thou art bound to believe, and to do, as they have promised for thee?

A. Yes verily; and by God's help so I will. And I heartily thank our heavenly Father, that he hath called me to this state of salvation, through Jesus Christ our Saviour. And I pray unto God to give me His grace, that I may continue in the same unto my life's end.

Catechist.—Rehearse the Articles of thy Belief.

A. I believe in God the Father Almighty, Maker of heaven and earth:

And in Jesus Christ his only Son our Lord, who was conceived by the Holy Ghost, born of the Virgin Mary, suffered under Pontius Pilate, was crucified, dead, and buried, He descended into hell; the third day he rose again from the dead, He ascended into heaven, and sitteth at the right hand of God the Father Almighty; from thence He shall come to judge the quick and the dead.

I believe in the Holy Ghost; the Holy Catholick Church; the Communion of Saints; the Forgiveness of Sins; the Resurrection of the Body; and the Life everlasting. Amen.

Q. What dost thou chiefly learn in these Articles of thy Belief?

A. First, I learn to believe in God the Father, who hath made me, and all the world.

Secondly, in God the Son, who hath redeemed me, and all mankind.

Thirdly, in God the Holy Ghost, who sanctifieth me, and all the elect people of God.

Q. You said, that your Godfathers and Godmothers did promise for you, that you should keep God's commandments. Tell me how many there be?

A. Ten.

Q. Which be they?

A. The same which God spake in the twentieth chapter of Exodus, saying, I am the Lord thy God, who brought thee out of the land of Egypt, out of the house of bondage.

I. Thou shalt have none other gods but me.

II. Thou shalt not make to thyself any graven image, nor the likeness of any thing that is in heaven above, or in the earth beneath, or in the water under the earth. Thou shalt not bow down to them, nor worship them: for I the Lord thy God am a jealous God, and visit the sins of the fathers upon the children, unto the third and fourth generation of them that hate Me, and shew mercy unto thousands of them that love Me, and keep My commandments.

III. Thou shalt not take the name of the Lord thy God in vain: for the Lord will not hold him guiltless that taketh His name in vain.

IV. Remember that thou keep holy the Sabbath-day. Six days shalt thou labour, and do all that thou hast to do; but the seventh day is the Sabbath of the Lord thy God. In it thou shalt do no manner of work, thou, and thy son, and thy daughter, thy man-servant, and thy maid-servant, thy cattle, and the stranger that is within thy gates. For in six days the Lord made heaven and earth, the sea, and all that in them is, and rested the seventh day; wherefore the Lord blessed the seventh day, and hallowed it.

V. Honour thy father and thy mother, that thy days may be long in the land which the Lord thy God giveth thee.

VI. Thou shalt do no murder.

VII. Thou shalt not commit adultery.

VIII. Thou shalt not steal.

IX. Thou shalt not bear false witness against thy neighbour.

X. Thou shalt not covet thy neighbour's house, thou shalt not covet thy neighbour's wife, nor his servant, nor his maid, nor his ox, nor his ass, nor any thing that is his.

Q. What dost thou chiefly learn by these commandments?

A. I learn two things: my duty towards God, and my duty towards my neighbour.

Q. What is thy duty towards God?

A. My duty towards God, is to believe in Him, to fear Him, and to love Him with all my heart, with all my mind, with all my soul, and with all my strength; to worship Him, to give Him thanks, to put my whole trust in Him, to call upon Him, to honour His holy name and His Word, and to serve Him truly all the days of my life.

Q. What is thy duty towards thy neighbour?

A. My duty towards my neighbour, is to love him as myself, and to do to all men as I would they should do unto me: to love, honour, and succour my father and mother: to honour and obey the Queen, and all that are put in authority under her: to submit myself to all my governours, teachers, spiritual pastors and masters: to order myself lowly and reverently to all my betters: to hurt no body by word nor deed: to be true and just in all my dealing: to bear no malice nor hatred in my heart: to keep my hands from picking and stealing, and my tongue from evil-speaking, lying, and slandering: to keep my body in temperance, soberness, and chastity: not to covet nor desire other men's goods, but to learn and labour truly to get mine own living, and to do my duty in that state of life unto which it shall please God to call me.

Catechist.—My good child, know this, that thou art not able to do these things of thyself, nor to walk in the commandments of God, and to serve Him, without His special grace; which thou must learn at all times to call for by diligent prayer. Let me hear, therefore, if thou canst say the Lord's Prayer.

A. Our Father, which art in heaven, hallowed be Thy name. Thy kingdom come. Thy will be done in earth, as it is in heaven. Give us this day our daily bread. And forgive us our trespasses, as we forgive them that trespass against us. And lead us not into temptation; but deliver us from evil. Amen.

Q. What desirest thou of God in this prayer?

A. I desire my Lord God our heavenly Father, who is the giver of all goodness, to send His grace unto me, and to all people; that we may worship Him, serve Him, and obey Him, as we ought to do. And·I pray unto God, that He will send us all things that be needful both for our souls and bodies; and that He will be merciful unto us, and forgive us our sins; and that it will please Him to save and defend us in all dangers ghostly and bodily; and that He will keep us from all sin and wickedness, and from our ghostly enemy, and from everlasting death. And this I trust He will do of His mercy and goodness, through our Lord Jesus Christ. And therefore I say, Amen, So be it.

Q. How many Sacraments hath Christ ordained in His Church?

A. Two only, as generally necessary to salvation—that is to say, Baptism, and the Supper of the Lord.

Q. What meanest thou by this word *Sacrament?*

A. I mean an outward and visible sign of an inward and spiritual grace given unto us, ordained by Christ Himself, as a means whereby we receive the same, and a pledge to assure us thereof.

Q. How many parts are there in a Sacrament?

A. Two; the outward visible sign, and the inward spiritual grace.

Q. What is the outward visible sign or form in Baptism?

A. Water; wherein the person is baptised *In the name of the Father, and of the Son, and of the Holy Ghost.*

Q. What is the inward and spiritual grace?

A. A death unto sin, and a new birth unto righteousness: for being by nature born in sin, and the children of wrath, we are hereby made the children of grace.

Q. What is required of persons to be baptized.

A. Repentance, whereby they forsake sin; and Faith, whereby they steadfastly believe the promises of God made to them in that Sacrament.

Q. Why then are infants baptized, when by reason of their tender age they cannot perform them?

A. Because they promise them both by their sureties; which promise, when they come to age, themselves are bound to perform.

Q. Why was the Sacrament of the Lord's Supper ordained?

A. For the continual remembrance of the sacrifice of the death of Christ, and of the benefits which we receive thereby.

Q. What it the outward part or sign of the Lord's Supper?

A. Bread and wine, which the Lord hath commanded to be received.

Q. What is the inward part, or thing signified?

A. The body and blood of Christ, which are verily and indeed taken and received by the faithful in the Lord's Supper.

Q. What are the benefits whereof we are partakers thereby?

A. The strengthening and refreshing of our souls by the body and blood of Christ, as our bodies are by the bread and wine.

Q. What is required of them who come to the Lord's Supper?

A. To examine themselves, whether they repent them truly of their former sins, steadfastly purposing to lead a new life; have a lively faith in God's mercy through Christ, with a thankful remembrance of His death; and be in charity with all men.

ARTICLES OF RELIGION.

I. *Of Faith in the Holy Trinity.*

There is but one living and true God, everlasting, without body, parts, or passions; of infinite power, wisdom, and goodness; the Maker and Preserver of all things, both visible and invisible. And in unity of this Godhead there be three Persons, of one substance, power, and eternity; the Father, the Son, and the Holy Ghost.

II. *Of the Word or Son of God, which was made very Man.*

The Son, which is the Word of the Father, begotten from everlasting of the Father, the very and eternal God, and of one substance with the Father, took man's nature in the womb of the blessed Virgin, of her substance; so that two whole and perfect natures, that is to say, the Godhead and Manhood, were joined together in one Person, never to be divided, whereof is one Christ, very God and very man; who truly suffered, was crucified, dead and buried, to reconcile His Father to us, and to be a sacrifice, not only for original guilt, but also for all actual sins of men.

III. *Of the going down of Christ into Hell.*

As Christ died for us, and was buried, so also is it to be believed, that He went down into hell.

IV. *Of the Resurrection of Christ.*

Christ did truly rise again from death, and took again His body, with flesh, bones, and all things appertaining to the perfection of man's nature; wherewith He ascended into heaven, and there sitteth, until He return to judge all men at the last day.

V. *Of the Holy Ghost.*

The Holy Ghost, proceeding from the Father and the Son, is of one substance, majesty, and glory, with the Father and the Son, very and eternal God.

VI. *Of the Sufficiency of the Holy Scriptures for Salvation.*

Holy Scripture containeth all things necessary to

salvation; so that whatsoever is not read therein, nor may be proved thereby, is not to be required of any man, that it should be believed as an article of the faith, or be thought requisite or necessary to salvation. In the name of the Holy Scripture we do understand those canonical books of the Old and New Testament, of whose authority was never any doubt in the Church.

Of the Names and Number of the Canonical Books.

Genesis,
Exodus,
Leviticus,
Numbers,
Deuteronomy,
Joshua,
Judges,
Ruth,
The First Book of Samuel,
The Second Book of Samuel,
The First Book of Kings,
The Second Book of Kings,
The First Book of Chronicles,
The Second Book of Chronicles,
The First Book of Esdras,
The Second Book of Esdras,
The Book of Esther,
The Book of Job,
The Psalms,
The Proverbs,
Ecclesiastes or Preacher,
Cantica, or Songs of Solomon,
Four Prophets the greater,
Twelve Prophets the less.

And the other Books (as *Hierome* saith) the Church doth read for example of life and instruction of manners ; but yet doth it not apply them to establish any doctrine. Such are these following :—

> The Third Book of Esdras,
> The Fourth Book of Esdras,
> The Book of Tobias,
> The Book of Judith,
> The rest of the Book of Esther,
> The Book of Wisdom,
> Jesus the Son of Sirach,
> Barach the Prophet,
> The Song of the Three Children,
> The Story of Susanna,
> Of Bel and the Dragon,
> The Prayer of Manasses,
> The First Book of Macabees,
> The Second Book of Macabees.

All the Books of the New Testament, as they are commonly received, we do receive, and account them canonical.

VII. *Of the Old Testament.*

The Old Testament is not contrary to the New ; for both in the Old and New Testament everlasting life is offered to mankind by Christ, who is the only Mediator between God and man, being both God and man. Wherefore they are not to be heard, which feign that the old fathers did look only for transitory promises. Although the law given from God by Moses, as touching ceremonies and rites, do not bind Christian men, nor the civil precepts thereof ought of necessity to be received in any commonwealth ; yet notwithstanding, no

Christian man whatsoever is free from the obedience of the commandments which are called moral.

VIII. *Of the Three Creeds.*

The Three Creeds, *Nicene* Creed, *Athanasius's* Creed, and that which is commonly called the *Apostles'* Creed, ought thoroughly to be received and believed; for they may be proved by most certain warrants of Holy Scripture.

IX. *Of Original or Birth-sin.*

Original Sin standeth not in the following of *Adam,* (as the *Pelagians* do vainly talk;) but it is the fault and corruption of the nature of every man, that naturally is ingendered of the offspring of *Adam;* whereby man is very far gone from original righteousness, and is of his own nature inclined *to* evil, so that the flesh lusteth always contrary to the spirit; and therefore in every person born into this world, it deserveth God's wrath and damnation. And this infection of nature doth remain, yea in them that are regenerated; whereby the lust of the flesh, called in Greek, *phronema sarkos,* which some do expound the wisdom, some sensuality, some the affection, some the desire, of the flesh, is not subject to the law of God. And although there is no condemnation for them that believe and are baptised, yet the Apostle doth confess, that concupiscence and lust hath of itself the nature of sin.

X. *Of Free-Will.*

The condition of man after the fall of *Adam* is such, that he cannot turn and prepare himself, by his own natural strength and good works, to faith, and calling

F

upon God: Wherefore we have no power to do good works pleasant and acceptable to God, without the grace of God by Christ preventing us, that we may have a good will, and working with us, when we have that good will.

XI. *Of the Justification of Man.*

We are accounted righteous before God, only for the merit of our Lord and Saviour Jesus Christ by Faith, and not for our own works or deservings: Wherefore, that we are justified by faith only is a most wholesome doctrine, and very full of comfort, as more largely is expressed in the Homily of Justification.

XII. *Of Good Works.*

Albeit that good works, which are the fruits of faith, and follow after justification, cannot put away our sins, and endure the severity of God's judgment; yet are they pleasing and acceptable to God in Christ, and do spring out necessarily of a true and lively faith; insomuch that by them a lively faith may be as evidently known as a tree discerned by the fruit.

XIII. *Of Works before Justification.*

Works done before the grace of Christ, and the inspiration of his Spirit, are not pleasant to God, forasmuch as they spring. not of faith in Jesus Christ, neither do they make men meet to receive grace, or (as the School-authors say) deserve grace of congruity: yea rather, for that they are not done as God hath willed and commanded them to be done, we doubt not but they have the nature of sin.

XIV. *Of Works of Supererogation.*

Voluntary works besides, over and above, God's commandments, which they call Works of Supererogation, cannot be taught without arrogancy and impiety; for by them men do declare, that they do not only render unto God as much as they are bound to do, but that they do more for his sake, than of bounden duty is required: whereas Christ saith plainly, When ye have done all that are commanded to you, say, we are unprofitable servants.

XV. *Of Christ alone without Sin.*

Christ in the truth of our nature was made like unto us in all things, sin only except, from which he was clearly void, both in his flesh, and in his spirit. He came to be the Lamb without spot, who, by sacrifice of himself once made, should take away the sins of the world, and sin, as Saint John saith, was not in him. But all we the rest, although baptised, and born again in Christ, yet offend in many things; and if we say we have no sin, we deceive ourselves, and the truth is not in us.

XVI. *Of Sin after Baptism.*

Not every deadly sin willingly committed after baptism is sin against the Holy Ghost, and unpardonable. Wherefore the grant of repentance is not to be denied to such as fall into sin after baptism. After we have received the Holy Ghost, we may depart from grace given, and fall into sin, and by the grace of God we may arise again, and amend our lives. And therefore they are to be condemned which say, they can no more sin as long as they live here, or deny the place of forgiveness to such as truly repent.

XVII. *Of Predestination and Election.*

Predestination to life is the everlasting purpose of God, whereby (before the foundations of the world were laid) he hath constantly decreed by his counsel secret to us, to deliver from curse and damnation those whom he hath chosen in Christ out of mankind, and to bring them by Christ to everlasting salvation, as vessels made to honour. Wherefore, they which be endued with so excellent a benefit of God be called according to God's purpose by his Spirit working in due season: they through grace obey the calling: they be justified freely: they be made sons of God by adoption: they be made like the image of his only-begotten Son Jesus Christ: they walk religiously in good works, and at length, by God's mercy, they attain to everlasting felicity.

As the godly consideration of predestination, and our election in Christ, is full of sweet, pleasant, and unspeakable comfort to godly persons, and such as feel in themselves the working of the Spirit of Christ, mortifying the works of the flesh, and their earthly members, and drawing up their mind to high and heavenly things, as well because it doth greatly establish and confirm their faith of eternal salvation to be enjoyed through Christ, as because it doth fervently kindle their love towards God: So, for curious and carnal persons, lacking the Spirit of Christ, to have continually before their eyes the sentence of God's predestination, is a most dangerous downfal, whereby the devil doth thrust them either into desperation, or into wretchlessness of most unclean living, no less perilous than desperation.

Furthermore, we must receive God's promises in such wise, as they be generally set forth to us in holy Scripture: and, in our doings, that will of God is to be followed, which we have expressly declared unto us in the Word of God.

XVIII. *Of obtaining eternal Salvation only by the Name of Christ.*

They also are to be had accursed that presume to say, That every man shall be saved by the Law or Sect which he professeth, so that he be diligent to frame his life according to that law, and the light of nature. For holy Scripture doth set out unto us only the name of Jesus Christ, whereby men must be saved.

XIX. *Of the Church.*

The visible church of Christ is a congregation of faithful men, in the which the pure Word of God is preached, and the sacraments be duly ministered according to Christ's ordinance in all those things that of necessity are requisite to the same.

As the Church of *Jerusalem, Alexandria,* and *Antioch* have erred, so also the Church of *Rome* hath erred, not only in their living and manner of ceremonies, but also in matters of faith.

XX. *Of the Authority of the Church.*

The Church hath power to decree Rites or Ceremonies, and authority in Controversies of Faith : and yet it is not lawful for the Church to ordain any thing that is contrary to God's Word written, neither may it so expound one place of Scripture that it be repugnant to another. Wherefore, although the Church be a witness and a keeper of holy writ, yet, as it ought not to decree any thing against the same, so besides the same ought it not to enforce any thing to be believed for necessity of salvation.

XXI. *Of the Authority of General Councils.*

General Councils may not be gathered together without the commandment and will of Princes. And when they be gathered together, (forasmuch as they be an assembly of men, whereof all be not governed with the Spirit and Word of God,) they may err, and sometimes have erred, even in things pertaining unto God. Wherefore things ordained by them as necessary to salvation have neither strength nor authority, unless it may be declared that they be taken out of holy Scripture.

XXII. *Of Purgatory.*

The Romish doctrine concerning Purgatory, Pardons, Worshipping, and Adoration, as well of Images as of Reliques, and also Invocation of Saints, is a fond thing vainly invented, and grounded upon no warranty of Scripture, but rather repugnant to the Word of God.

XXIII. *Of Ministering in the Congregation.*

It is not lawful for any man to take upon him the office of public preaching, or ministering the Sacraments in the congregation, before he be lawfully called, and sent to execute the same. And those we ought to judge lawfully called and sent, which be chosen and called to this work by men who have public authority given unto them in the congregation, to call and send ministers into the Lord's vineyard.

XXIV. *Of speaking in the Congregation in such a tongue as the people understandeth.*

It is a thing plainly repugnant to the Word of God, and the custom of the Primitive Church, to have public prayer in the Church, or to minister the Sacraments in a tongue not understanded of the people.

XXV. *Of the Sacraments.*

Sacraments ordained of Christ be not only badges or tokens of Christian men's profession, but rather they be certain sure witnesses, and effectual signs of grace, and God's god-will towards us, by the which he doth work invisibly in us, and doth not only quicken, but also strengthen and confirm our faith in Him.

There are two Sacraments ordained of Christ our Lord in the Gospel, that is to say, Baptism, and the Supper of the Lord.

Those five commonly called Sacraments, that is to say, Confirmation, Penance, Orders, Matrimony, and extreme Unction, are not to be counted for Sacraments of the Gospel, being such as have grown partly of the corrupt following of the apostles, partly are states of life allowed in the Scriptures, but yet have not like nature of Sacraments with Baptism and the Lord's Supper, for that they have not any visible sign or ceremony ordained of God.

The Sacraments were not ordained of Christ to be gazed upon, or to be carried about, but that we should duly use them. And in such only as worthily receive the same they have a wholesome effect or operation, but they that receive them unworthily purchase to themselves damnation, as Saint *Paul* saith.

XXVI. *Of the Unworthiness of the Ministers, which hinders not the effect of the Sacrament.*

Although in the visible Church the evil be ever mingled with the good, and sometimes the evil have chief authority in the ministration of the Word and

Sacraments, yet forasmuch as they do not the same in their own name, but in Christ's, and do minister by His commission and authority, we may use their ministry, both in hearing the Word of God and in the receiving of the Sacraments. Neither is the effect of Christ's ordinance taken away by their wickedness, nor the grace of God's gifts diminished from such as by faith and rightly do receive the Sacraments ministered unto them; which be effectual, because of Christ's institution and promise, although they be ministered by evil men.

Nevertheless, it appertaineth to the discipline of the Church that inquiry be made of evil ministers, and that they be accused by those that have knowledge of their offences; and finally, being found guilty, by just judgment be deposed.

XXVII. *Of Baptism.*

Baptism is not only a sign of profession, and mark of difference, whereby Christian men are discerned from others that be not christened, but it is also a sign of regeneration or new birth, whereby, as by an instrument, they that receive baptism rightly are grafted into the Church; the promises of the forgiveness of sin, and of our adoption to be the sons of God by the Holy Ghost, are visibly signed and sealed; faith is confirmed, and grace increased by virtue of prayer unto God. The baptism of young children is in any wise to be retained in the Church, as most agreeable with the institution of Christ.

XXVIII. *Of the Lord's Supper.*

The Supper of the Lord is not only a sign of the love that Christians ought to have among themselves one to another, but rather it is a Sacrament of our redemption by Christ's death; insomuch that to such as rightly, worthily, and with faith, reĉeive the same, the bread which we break is a partaking of the body of Christ; and likewise, the cup of blessing is a partaking of the blood of Christ.

Transubstantiation (or the change of the substance of bread and wine) in the Supper of the Lord, cannot be proved by holy writ, but it is repugnant to the plain words of Scripture, overthroweth the nature of a Sacrament, and hath given occasion to many superstitions.

The body of Christ is given, taken, and eaten, in the Supper, only after an heavenly and spiritual manner. And the mean whereby the body of Christ is received and eaten in the Supper is faith.

The Sacrament of the Lord's Supper was not by Christ's ordinance reserved, carried about, lifted up, or worshipped.

XXIX. *Of the Wicked which eat not the Body of Christ in the use of the Lord's Supper.*

The wicked, and such as be void of a lively faith, although they do carnally and visibly press with their teeth (as Saint *Augustine* saith) the Sacrament of the body and blood of Christ, yet in no wise are they partakers of Christ; but rather, to their condemnation, do eat and drink the sign or sacrament of so great a thing.

XXX. *Of both kinds.*

The cup of the Lord is not to be denied to the lay-people; for both the parts of the Lord's Sacrament, by Christ's ordinance and commandment, ought to be ministered to all Christian men alike.

XXXI. *Of the one Oblation of Christ finished upon the Cross.*

The offering of Christ once made is that perfect redemption, propitiation, and satisfaction, for all the sins of the whole world, both original and actual; and there is none other satisfaction for sin, but that alone. Wherefore the sacrifices of masses, in the which it was commonly said that the priest did offer Christ for the quick and the dead, to have remission of pain or guilt, were blasphemous fables and dangerous deceits.

XXXII. *Of the Marriage of Priests.*

Bishops, priests, and deacons, are not commanded by God's law either to vow the estate of single life or to abstain from marriage: therefore it is lawful also for them, as for all other Christian men, to marry at their own discretion, as they shall judge the same to serve better to godliness.

XXXIII. *Of excommunicate Persons, how they are to be avoided.*

That persons which, by open denunciation of the Church, is rightly cut off from the unity of the Church, and excommunicated, ought to be taken of the whole multitude of the faithful as an heathen and publican, until he be openly reconciled by penance, and received into the Church by a judge that hath authority thereunto.

XXXIV. *Of the Traditions of the Church.*

It is not necessary that traditions and ceremonies be in all places one, or utterly like; for at all times they have been divers, and may be changed according to the diversities of countries, times, and men's manners, so that nothing be ordained against God's Word. Whosoever, through his private judgment, willingly and purposely, doth openly break the traditions and ceremonies of the Church, which be not repugnant to the Word of God, and be ordained and approved by common authority, ought to be rebuked openly (that others may fear to do the like), as he that offendeth against the common order of the Church, and hurteth the authority of the magistrate, and woundeth the consciences of the weak brethren.

Every particular or national Church hath authority to ordain, change, and abolish, ceremonies or rites of the Church, ordained only by man's authority, so that all things be done to edifying.

XXXV. *Of Homilies.*

The Second Book of Homilies, the several titles whereof we have joined under this Article, doth contain a godly and wholesome doctrine, and necessary for these times, as doth the former Book of Homilies, which were set forth in the time of *Edward* the Sixth; and therefore we judge them to be read in churches by the ministers, diligently and distinctly, that they may be understanded of the people.

Of the Names of the Homilies.

1. Of the right Use of the Church.
2. Against peril of Idolatry.
3. Of the repairing and keeping clean of Churches.
4. Of good Works : first of Fasting.
5. Against Gluttony and Drunkenness.
6. Against Excess of Apparel.

7. Of Prayer.
8. Of the Place and Time of Prayer.
9. That Common Prayers and Sacraments ought to be ministered in a known tongue.
10. Of the reverend estimation of God's Word.
11. Of Alms-doing.
12. Of the Nativity of Christ.
13. Of the Passion of Christ.
14. Of the Resurrection of Christ.
15. Of the worthy receiving of the Sacrament of the Body and Blood of Christ.
16. Of the Gifts of the Holy Ghost.
17. For the Rogation-days.
18. Of the state of Matrimony.
19. Of Repentance.
20. Against Idleness.
21. Against Rebellion.

XXXVI. *Of Consecration of Bishops and Ministers.*

The Book of Consecration of Archbiships and Bishops, and ordering of Priests and Deacons, lately set forth in the time of *Edward* the Sixth, and confirmed at the same time by authority of Parliament, doth contain all things necessary to such consecration and ordering : neither hath it any thing that of itself is superstitious and ungodly. And therefore whosoever are consecrated or ordered according to the rites of that book, since the second year of the forenamed King *Edward* unto this time, or hereafter shall be consecrated or ordered according to the same rites; we decree all such to be rightly, orderly, and lawfully consecrated and ordered.

XXXVII. *Of the Civil Magistrates.*

The Queen's Majesty hath the chief power in this realm of *England*, and other her dominions, unto whom the chief government of all estates of this realm, whether they be ecclesiastical or civil, in all causes doth appertain, and is not, nor ought to be, subject to any foreign jurisdiction.

Where we attribute to the Queen's Majesty the chief government, by which titles we understand the minds of some slanderous folks to be offended, we give not to our princes the ministering either of God's Word or of the Sacraments, the which thing the injunctions also lately set forth by *Elizabeth* our Queen do most plainly testify; but that only prerogative, which we see to have been given always to all godly princes in Holy Scriptures by God Himself; that is, that they should rule all estates and degrees committed to their charge by God, whether they be ecclesiastical or temporal, and restrain with the civil sword the stubborn and evil-doers.

The Bishop of *Rome* hath no jurisdiction in this realm of *England*.

The laws of the realm may punish Christian men with death, for heinous and grievous offences.

It is lawful for Christian men, at the commandment of the magistrate, to wear weapons and serve in the wars.

XXXVIII. *Of Christian men's Goods, which are not common.*

The riches and goods of Christians are not common, as touching the right, title, and possession of the same, as certain Anabaptists do falsely boast. Notwithstanding, every man ought, of such things as he possesseth, liberally to give alms to the poor, according to his ability.

XXXIX. *Of a Christian man's oath.*

As we confess that vain and rash swearing is forbidden Christian men by our Lord Jesus Christ and *James* His apostle, so we judge that Christian religion doth not prohibit, but that a man may swear when the magistrate requireth, in a cause of faith and charity, so it be done according to the prophet's teaching, in justice, judgement, and truth.

SYNOPSIS

OF

ECCLESIASTICAL HISTORY.

PART I.

PRELIMINARY OBSERVATIONS AND ORIGIN OF ECCLE-SIASTICAL HISTORY—PROPAGATION OF CHRISTIAN-ITY — MORAL AND PHYSICAL STATE OF PRIMITIVE CHRISTIANITY.

Ecclesiastical or Church History is the narration of events connected with the career of the society of men believing in God's revelation by Christ.   Our word Church is derived from two Greek words, kuriou, oikia, the Lord's house, hence the meaning of a place set apart

for the worship of God. The word ecclesiastical is
derived from a Greek verb ekkalein, to call forth, allud-
ing to an assembly of Greeks called out upon due
authority. In the New Testament it has various significations : 1. The whole body of the faithful. 2. The
invisible Church. 3. Any congregation of worshippers
of God the Father, through God the Son. 4. The place
of worship.—(Matt. xvi. 18 ; Eph. v. 27 ; Acts viii. 1 ;
xi. 26).

The four Gospels bring down the history to the year
33 A.D. ; the Acts of the Apostles from 33 to 63 A.D.
The Fathers, Clement of Rome, Barnabas, Hermas, of the
1st century; Ignatius, Polycarp, Justin Martyr, Nenæus,
and Dionysius of Corinth, in the 2nd century ; Clement
of Alexandria, Tertullian, Origen, Cyprian, Gregory
Thaumaturgus, in the 3rd. Hegesippus, a Jewish convert, A.D. 170, and Eusebius, who was born at Cæsarea
in Palestine about 270 A.D.

The empire of Rome was the whole civilized world
at that time known under Augustus, in whose reign our
Saviour was born. Great rapidity of communication—
the general knowledge of the Greek language throughout the eastern, and of the Latin throughout the western
portion of the empire—the mild government of the more
distant portion of the empire—the contempt for religion
in general beyond its usefulness as a political instrument—
the consequent infidelity of the educated heathen, and
the general immorality—were in some senses favourable
conditions for advancing the faith of Christ. Although
the country of the Jews was nominally tributary to Rome,
they had, as King of Judea, Herod an Idumæan. He
extirpated the Maccabees, oppressed the people, and
was the cause of general licentiousness throughout th
kingdom.

The great sects of the Jews were the Pharisees (from Pharash, to divide from); the Sadducees, who derived their name from Sadoc, a follower of Sochœus, president of the Jewish Sanhedrim, B.C. 250. The Essenes, a kind of speculative and ascetic sect, not mentioned in Scriptures. The Scribes, copiers, and afterwards expounders of the law. Caballists, a mystic sect of interpretators of the law according to an arithmetic power of the letters, which composed every word in it. Herodians, a political sect attached to the Herods. Galileans, a faction opposed to them. The Jews had to a certain extent their religious rights and laws under the Sanhedrim and High Priesthood, but increasing numbers caused many to emigrate into all parts of the Roman empire, and thus a strange mixture of Roman and Judaical rites and manners were blended together, not only in Judea, but in other neighbouring parts of the Roman dominions in the East. Both the Jews and the Gentiles were in expectation of the Messias—the former as a temporal ruler, and the latter as some great one to come from the East. In the 35th year of Herod, called the Great, Zacharias a priest was informed by divine authority, that his son John should be the forerunner of Christ. This John, surnamed the Baptist, reproved Herod Antipas for a wicked life, and was beheaded by him A.D. 30. Christ was born one year afterwards at Bethlehem, whither Joseph and the Virgin mother were obliged to proceed, in obedience to the edict on property, their usual residence being at Nazareth. He was circumcised the eighth day, and presented in the temple forty days after birth, when the Virgin offered sacrifice according to the law of Moses on her purification; on which occasion Simon and Anna, devotees of the temple in Jerusalem, by divine inspiration, acknowledged the infant Christ.

Herod, on ascertaining the arrival of certain Gentile governors or learned men, called Magi, from the land of Arabia, demanding the King of the Jews, whose birth was made known by the guiding star, was alarmed: fearing the coming of the great temporal Prince expected by the Jews, he sent forth and slew the infants in Bethlehem from two years old and under. Joseph and the Blessed Virgin fled to Egypt, and did not return to Nazareth until the death of Herod. John the Baptist received the Saviour at the age of thirty, to the rite of baptism, lest he should have seemed to have neglected the due observance of all righteous ceremonies. The subsequent history of our Lord must be searched for in the Gospels, as we have to do only with the strictly historical account of the Church. Herod, shortly after the birth of Christ, died under the visitation of divine wrath, and his kingdom was divided among his three sons. Archelaus was, in the 10th year of his reign, banished by the Emperor Augustus, and his dominions reduced under the charge of a governor or procurator. Pontius Pilate held that office at the time of our Lord's death. It was not till A.D. 8 that Judea, as a part of the whole empire which had been ordered to be taxed, was laid under contribution. From that time, the Romans were undisguised masters at Jerusalem, and the High Priest was appointed by Rome.

A few months after our Lord's commencing his ministry, he made choice of twelve apostles as his chosen companions. Within a year they were sufficiently instructed, although poor and unlearned men, to announce the Gospel, working of miracles and preaching repentance and faith in Christ. As twelve was the number of the tribes, so the seventy assisting ministers, mentioned only by St Luke (x. 1) were numbered according to the members of the Sanhedrim. They were to go only to places where the Saviour was to follow; the twelve went at large to any of the cities of Israel.

The Church is spoken of by Christ, in the words addressed to St Peter, the oldest of the apostles, in the future tense; but after the descent of the gift of tongues at Pentecost, we read for the first time of the actual existence of the Church.—Acts ii. 42.

The working of miracles, actions more than human, were the permitted means of enforcing doctrines so powerfully, that earnest and humble converts were daily increased. And above all, the gift of declaring in foreign tongues the wonderful works of God in Christ; for since at the time of the descent of tongues many strangers were in Jerusalem, the converts carried the elements of Christian doctrine into various parts of the empire, and probably the churches of Ephesus, Smyrna, Athens, Corinth, Rome, and Alexandria, were one by one soon founded, through the determined energy of the church at Jerusalem and Antioch, though in a more formal sense they were not completed. The first idea of a formal unity of belief is mentioned in Acts ii. 42, and is essentially the same held to this day by the Anglican Church. 1. Baptism. 2. Unity in apostles' teaching. 3. Eucharistic sacrifice and reception. 4. Public and uniform prayer. The poor were first to accept the Gospel, and consequently their necessities were supplied from the richer converts. Nevertheless, entire community of goods was never practised. This Church system, so agreeable to the constitution of the Anglican, undoubtedly possessed a liturgical service, as implied in the words of St Paul, "the cup of blessing which we bless." St Chrysostom alludes to a *formulary* in his gloss on the passage in 1 Cor. xiv. 16. The expressions of Pliny, in his letter to the Emperor Trajan, sufficiently prove that a form of prayer was used by the Christian Church in the first century ; at the same time, it is probable that extempore prayer was used also. Hymns were sung by choristers appointed for the purpose. (See *Bingham's Christian Antiquities*).

The primitive Church (some say not until the 3rd century) seemed to consider her teaching with reference to the necessities of two portions of the people—the preparing of catechumens and those grounded and rooted in the faith, or the faithful, which condition was arrived at by instruction after baptism. The latter were sent forth into the world to spread the doctrine they were instructed in, so that constant opposition arose from the false religions of the time, thus Peter and John, after healing a cripple at the Beautiful gate of the temple, were, at the instance of the Sadducees, imprisoned by the Roman governor of the tower of Antonia, overlooking Jerusalem. The Pharisees, reconciling their consciences to truth and falsehood by ritual strictness, the Sadducees by speculative philosophy, and the Pagans from political motives, and fear of a purer form of religion than theirs, which sanctioned every bestial immorality, even as seen from the testimony of their own writers (Seneca de Irâ, ii. 8)—were all opposed to the new teaching. For such a religion as Christ's, nothing but persecution, like that of wolves on sheep, could be expected. Still there were favourable circumstances which at all tir

more or less, operated as correctives of the persecuting
spirit. The fierce jealousy of the rival sects restrained
the hands of the Jewish leaders, th e indifference of the
Roman to what he regarded as Jewish squabbles about
religion, and the desire of all the principal men for
peace and tranquillity, which were the principles
of the New Testament, assisted the development of
Christianity. Be it as it may, by the aid of Divine and
miraculous power, the devotion of missionaries, and the
learning and morals of the Christian leaders, the Christian religion rapidly advanced. At first, the numbers
increased so much that seven deacons had to be appointed
as assistants of the apostles; they were confined to the
performance of some ecclesiastical and civil duties, and
did not possess the power of conferring supernatural
gifts. As the early Church was governed by divinely
inspired men, that fact is sufficient for all useful purposes to prove that the episcopal form of government
was the model to ages after that period. The first
bishop of Jerusalem, James the less, ruled for thirty
years, with the title of the Just. After his martyrdom,
his brother Simeon succeeded him, and a regular chain
and authority existed through the first fifteen bishops
of the *circumcision* down to *Marcus*, the first *Gentile*
bishop in 135 A.D. The duties of a bishop or presiding
governor of a diocese, were only altered in accordance
with the necessary variations of nations and people, and
at first, Theodoret, a renowned writer in his gloss on
1 Tim. iii. 1, admits that the names bishop and presbyter were anciently alike; those now called bishops
were called apostles. The name of apostle was however set apart for the twelve apostles chosen by our
Lord, and the name bishop retained for those who had

been called apostles. Ignatius, a disciple of St John, is plain and explicit upon the authority and divinely constituted succession of bishops to the apostles. Subsequently, as the Christian religion spread into the country, there were assistant bishops called Chorepiscopi or Suffragans added, who, however, could not confirm, and were supported, as were all the ministers, by the offertory of the people. (See *Bingham's Christian Antiquities*). The bishop was sometimes called upon to exercise his extreme power of excommunication (Tit. iii. 10); the further punishment of "anathema" (1 Cor. v. 5, 1 Tim. i. 20), delivered up the impenitent to Satan without Church prayers or benefit of sacrament. Tertullian and Irenæus mention the undoubted practice of the sacrament of baptism being administered not only to adults but to children; and rivers and open places, till the frequency of persecution drove Christians into houses, were the ordinary places of baptism.

Stephen, who converted and baptised many people, was the first victim of the malice of the unbelieving Jews; having, in a dispute with the five synagogues, baffled them by aid of the Divine wisdom. As this violence was perpetrated without the cognizance of the Roman governor, it is evident, that in matters of religious differences, the Romans sometimes regarded a popular tumult as a kind of safety valve for that indignation which their exactions and tyrannies excited.

The persecution carried out by Saul of Tarsus against the Christians, is a proof how little the civil power of Rome interfered in these matters. Among those who were members of the five synagogues (Cilicia being one), was Saul of Tarsus. Hitherto the Church had not suffered much from external violence; but the per-

secuting spirit which was fanned into violence by Saul,
obliged many to flee, and so carried into distant parts
of the empire the elements of the Gospel of Christ.
Among them was Philip the deacon, who was driven to
Samaria; as it had been mentioned by Christ, and
was in some sense Jewish, the practice of the apostles,
to confine their missionary efforts to their countrymen
was not broken. Hence arose the rite of confirmation
(see Acts viii). Simon the sorcerer, requesting the
Holy Ghost at the hands of the apostles, who had
been sent from Jerusalem to confirm the converts, was
the origin of the modern term " Simony," an unlawful
contract for presenting a cleric to a benefice. He was,
on refusal, angered into becoming an opponent of
Christian doctrine, and originator of Gnosticism, the
greatest heresy which the Church has ever had to
oppose. Heresy signifies obstinate denial of doctrine,
clearly revealed in Sacred Scripture: schism, division
from the discipline of the Church. St Paul mentions
the earliest heretics and schismatics by name, so that
even in his time, division began, though with no great
success, saving and except in the Gnostic error.

Elementary forms of error, touching the nature and
origin of evil, gained a footing in the middle of the
first century, rising gradually into the distinction of a
philosophy that had the name of Gnostic attached.
The first century saw the beginning of error taught
by those who mingled Christianity and Judaism, as the
Nazarenes and Ebionites—others grafted into Christian
doctrine the eastern philosophy or Gnosticism, such
were Cerinthus and Menander. To oppose these and
the like heretics, the early Church had ministers whose
office was never revived in modern times, namely Evan-

gelists and Prophets. In the face of every opposition the Church flourished exceedingly, some occurrences being in their favour, as for instance when the Jews in the reign of Caligula, who succeeded Tiberius, were so frightened by the order for setting up his image as God in the temple, that they were diverted from all thoughts of persecution. That many churches were founded or increased during this interval of peace, there is no doubt; and in Antioch, where the name of Christian was first heard, arose the element of the Gentile church, the celebrated Ignatius succeeding Evodius as the bishop in the year 70.

At Antioch arose, during St Paul's first apostolic journey, the question as to the necessity of conversion to Mosaic institutions, taught by Jewish converts. The first council of the Christian Church was held upon this question at Jerusalem. There were present St James, St Peter, St John, St Paul, St Barnabas, and presbyters—St James presiding. They gave sentence against the teaching of the Jewish Christians. Epiphanius tells us, that Cerinthus was the ringleader of the disturbance at Antioch, and afterwards was the first to teach the heresy called after his name, A.D. 46. Eight years after this, Nero became Emperor of Rome, and was the first emperor that persecuted the Christian Church. In his reign St Paul was taken prisoner, A.D. 64, in a tumult at Jerusalem, and having appealed as a Roman citizen to the Emperor, was sent to Rome, resided there two years, and was set at liberty on being found innocent of any opposition to the Roman law. St Peter joined St Paul at Rome, as his associate in organizing the Church there, the care of which they committed to Linus, the first bishop. But of all the patriarchal churches of Rome, Antioch, Jerusalem, and

Alexandria—the last was most remarkable. Thence
arose the Therapeutæ, a religious sect established,
according to Eusebius, by St Mark; and there was
translated the Septuagint version of the Old Testament.

We now come to an important period of the Christian history, because, after the destruction of Jerusalem
by Titus (A.D. 69), the son and successor of Vespasian,
it is most difficult to ascertain the truth of the facts related. Upwards of a million Jews were destroyed in the
siege and subsequent capture, though all the Christians
are said to have escaped to Pella, accompanied by Simeon
their bishop. Here the Nazarenes, a name at first given
to all Christians, and subsequently to judaizing Christians and Ebionites, vexed the unity of the Church.
Menander also about the same time broached a heresy
called after his name, arrogating to himself the character
of an Œon, or special emanation of the Deity. Yet the
troubles consequent upon these heresies were as nothing
to the cruel persecution of Christians by Domitian, the
successor of the amiable Titus. The Jews were frequently confounded with the Christians in these persecutions. In this reign St John, who was banished to
Patmos, an isle in the Ægean Sea, wrote the Book of
Revelation. In the first chapter, he mentions the heresy
of the Nicolaitans, who were supposed to have licensed
evil conduct rather than errors of faith; by some they
are accused of Gnosticism. Nerva succeeded Domitian
A.D. 97, and in that year Timothy, bishop of Ephesus,
suffered martyrdom in a public tumult. St John, taking
advantage of the peaceful edicts of Nerva to the Jews
and Christians, returned to Ephesus, dying there at the
age of 100 years, in the reign of Trajan, having, as
supposed, sanctioned the present collection of the New
Testament writings. This was the last of the apostles,

and to him succeeded, among the writers of early Christianity, Clemens, bishop of Rome; Ignatius, a disciple of St John, bishop of Antioch 70 A.D.; Polycarp, bishop of Smyrna, appointed by St John 82 A.D.; and Hermas, companion of St Paul (Rom. xvi. 4); as well as Barnabas, who wrote an epistle of little worth and not canonical. Antioch was the first church in point of rank and power of the first century. Afterwards it was surpassed by Alexandria. From Syria to the shores of the Black Sea, throughout the provinces of Asia Minor, along the coasts of the Ægean Sea, and the leading established cities of Greece—in fine, throughout the greatest part of Europe, Asia, and Africa, to the farthest Indies, in spite of heresies, schism, and persecution, the Christian Church flourished and extended; but ere the second century is well reached into, the chief cause of success, the exhibition of miraculous powers, gradually died out.

We may, for the sake of seeing how very nearly the Church of England agrees, in spirit if not in letter, with the primitive Church, rapidly sketch the rites, doctrines, and ceremonies of the period included in the first 150 years.

Church of England or Anglican.

1. The Church founded, and called Christians at Antioch.

1. The Church of England, as she reformed herself, is described in the 19th Article.

2. Missionaries preached Christ.

2. Laymen may preach Christ—as schoolmasters, Scripture readers, &c., though not to minister in sacred rites.

3. Apostles ruled.

3. Bishops rule.

4. The written Scriptures (Old Testament, and afterwards portions of New Testament) were read in the congregation.

4. Scriptures read, Old and New entirely, with sermons to explain them.

5. Admission by baptism (generally of adults), and by immersion.

5. Baptism regenerates, and admits into Christ's body.

6. Life by sacrament of the Lord's Supper, after the Agapæ or love feasts.

6. The Lord's Supper, the strength and refreshment of the soul.

7. Excommunication the only mode of punishment and power.

7. Excommunication the only weapon of the Anglican Church.

8. Festivals were Sundays, Easter, and Pentecost only.

8. Same festivals, and a few others kept in the same spirit; and only those of the three first centuries.

9. Fasts, Good Friday only.

9. Fasts added, but only of the three first centuries, according to the power of the Church to do so.

10. No creeds, but the written Epistles and Three Gospels, or portions of faith delivered on the authority of individual bishops — Apostles' Creed, fourth century.

10. Creeds—three of the whole Church.

11. The clergy were bishops or presiding elders, presbyters, besides lay-deacons and deaconesses.

11. Clergy and laity separate.

12. Miraculous power.

12. Miracles gradually ceased after the first century.

What is Ecclesiastical History?

Derive the word Church?

What are its significations in the New Testament?

What are the sources of Ecclesiastical History?

What were the favourable conditions for the advance of Christianity under the Roman empire?

Give some account of the Pharisees and other sects?

Was there any expectation of the Messiah at the time of His birth?

When was Christ born?

Relate some details?

What was the course determined on by Herod?

When did Herod die, and how was the kingdom of Judea divided?

Who was Pontius Pilate?

What probable cause was there for the choice of twelve disciples, and the assisting ministers?

What difference was there in their authority and mission?

In what way did our Saviour address St Peter touching the Church?

What were the honourable means of spreading Christianity?

Which were the primitive Churches?

What grounds are there for supposing that a liturgical form was extant in the early Church?

When was the division of the congregations into catechumens and faithful first arranged?

How did circumstances stand in favour of St Peter and St John in their mission?

What order was found necessary to be instituted by the Church as she increased?

How were they distinguished from the apostles in authority and mission?

Who was first bishop of Jerusalem?

Can we trace a succession there?

What is the testimony of Theodoret? and Ignatius?

What was at first the practice with regard to baptism?

Who was St Stephen?

What was the consequence of his martyrdom?

How was Cilicia remarkable?

Give some account of Simon Magus?

What is the difference between heresy and schism?

What is remarkable with regard to those errors?

Who probably first introduced error into the primitive Church as a system?

What orders were there in the primitive Church now discontinued?

What circumstance was favourable to the Christians during the reign of Caligula?

Who was Ignatius?

Give some account of the first Council at Jerusalem?

Who was the first Emperor that persecuted the Christian Church?

What befel St Paul in that Emperor's reign?

Who was first bishop of Rome?

Give some account of the Therapeutæ?

Where did they spring from?

When and by whom was Jerusalem destroyed?

PART II.

HISTORY OF THE CHRISTIAN CHURCH FROM THE SECOND CENTURY TO THE DECLINE OF PAGANISM.

PLINY, the Proprætor of Pontus, wrote a letter to the Emperor Trajan, in the beginning of the second century, asking for instruction concerning the amazing progress of Christianity, in which epistle the morality, the litur- ‌ical form of Christian worship, and the eucharistic

sacrifices, were alluded to. Towards the end of this
emperor's reign, Saturninus began to teach heretical
doctrines in the churches of Syria, Basilides likewise at
Alexandria, and Elxus in Palestine — all leading to
Gnostic errors and wild unsettled theories. But in the
reign of Hadrian, Emperor of Rome, who rebuilt
Jerusalem, the Christians, who were known to have
refused to join a revolt of the Jews, were, upon the
utter dispersion of that nation by Julius Severus, in
135, allowed to remain at Jerusalem. This was of
invaluable service to the Church, torn as it had been by
the various heresies and schisms which seem to exist
even side by side with the truth. Hadrian also issued
a decree favourable to the Christians, as it required
violation of the laws before any could accuse them, and
provided a penalty against false accusers, and thus pre-
vented the mob demanding the immolation of a Christian at the public games. Celsus, a learned philo-
sopher in Hadrian's reign, attacked, in a treatise on
Truth, the Christian religion; which was, however,
admirably defended by Origen. Following Celsus in
some of his opinions was Carpocrates, the first asserter
of the simple humanity of Jesus. But Valentinus,
an Egyptian, disappointed of a bishopric, taught doctrines far more dangerous to Christianity than any
previously set forth, and diffused them through Europe,
Africa, and Asia. Tertullian, Irenæus, and Clement
of Alexandria, wrote against him. Cerdon and Marcion
about the same time taught heresy, and rejected the
whole of the Old Testament and the New, except the
ten Epistles of St Paul. But as these heresies always
excited Christian philosophers to reply, so at times
they might have been the means of drawing forth

eminent men from the obscure and doubtful pursuit
of Eastern philosophy to search Christian truth.
Among such was the eminent Justin, whose apology for
Christianity, after his conversion to it, was the cause of
the Emperor Antoninus Pius issuing an edict in favour
of it. But scarcely had peace existed for a short interval, when, in the reign of this emperor, there arose between the Eastern and Western Churches the celebrated
controversy, whether Easter should be kept according
to the Eastern rule, on the authority of St John and
Philip, on the third day after the 14th of March; or
whether, according to the Western Churches, citing St
Paul as their authority, all Christians should put off
their paschal feast until the evening preceding the festal
day of the resurrection, which was the nearest Sunday to
the full moon of Nisan, the first Jewish month. The
Eastern and Western Churches were both in communion
with each other at that time, and a discussion between
Anicetus, bishop of Rome, and Polycarp, bishop of
Smyrna, ensued, without any effectual result, till Victor,
then succeeding bishop of Rome, declared excommunication against Polycrates, bishop of Ephesus, who then
headed the opposition of the Eastern Church. Nor was
it till the Council of Nice 325, that the Western custom
obtained. This was the first intimation of a supremacy
assumed by the Church of Rome over the Eastern
Church. Hegesippus at this time was an ecclesiastical
writer of some importance, a small portion of his
works is preserved by Eusebius. Many heretical
teachers, and many defenders of the faith, were living
at this time. Among the former was Montanus, A.D.
168, who pretended to inspiration, and taught that a
severe ascetic life was necessary to salvation; among

the latter, Theophilus of Antioch, and Dionysius of
Corinth, who was converted by reading the Sacred
Scriptures. In the year 177 arose a fierce persecution
at Lyons and Vienne, in Gaul. During this, Irenæus,
a presbyter of Lyons, was dispatched with a letter to
Eleutherus, bishop of Rome, touching his inclination
to Montanism. From which incident one fact is
evident—viz., the exceeding breadth and latitude of
the early Church upon orthodoxy—for even Barde-
sanes, holding Gnostic error, was allowed to be on great
points orthodox : so a foreign bishop sends an affec-
tionate letter from his church to warn and persuade
the chief bishop of the West. The absence of Irenæus
proved his safety. He afterwards became bishop of
Lyons, and wrote five books against heresy. From
this Eleutherus bishop of Rome, it is supposed that
Lucius, a British chief, obtained instruction in the
Latin language, the language of the civilized world, as
well as directions for the government of the British
Church. Thus Christian doctrines, it may be supposed,
had prevailed already to a certain extent, but order
and discipline were much wanted, and the two missionaries sent over by Eleutherus rapidly extended the
gospel in Britain.

The thirteenth bishop of Rome, Victor, after once
assuming the power of excommunicating a foreign
bishop, was prepared to go to any length in keeping it.
Irenæus opposed his pretensions of rule over his
Church with a candour and gentleness worthy of all
admiration.

Parts of the great work of Irenæus, called " A Refu-
tation of Knowledge, falsely so called," are extant in
the original Greek, and there is an original Latin ver

sion of the whole. In that work, he states that "*we can name the men the apostles made bishops in their several churches, appointing them their successors.*" *It proves the undoubted form of Episcopacy in the early Church as a divine institution, so far as the apostles arranged that form of government.*

About the end of the second century, one Theodotus of Byzantium, a tanner, on asserting the simple humanity of Christ as an excuse for having denied Christ during the persecution under Severus the twenty-first Emperor of Rome, and Artemon, by whose name the heresy was generally known, were excomunicated by Victor, bishop of Rome. Natalus, a disciple, was made a bishop of this heretical church; but lived to avow his error.

It is worthy of remark, that a synod of bishops, priests and deacons, was convened at Antioch in 269, to take cognizance of the error to which Paul of Samosata, bishop of Antioch, had become a convert. Having resisted the sentence of deprivation pronounced by the synod, the Emperor Aurelian, on the application of the synod, enforced their sentence, which was the first instance of temporal interference in the spiritual matters of the early Church. This error soon branched out into further errors on the doctrine of the Trinity, which appeared first in a tangible form in the writings of Praxeas, a Greek. Tertullian soon answered him, repeating nearly as we have it, the Apostles' Creed, as the faith handed down to the Church from the first — *an historical evidence of inestimable force and use.* The heresy of Praxeas was followed fifty years subsequently by that of Sabellius, whose followers were called Patripassians, as their error made the Father to suffer on the cross. The early Church had suffered no open secession, and the creed was in great measure uncorrupted. The earliest records show that the Eucharist was administered frequently; that baptism was administered to infants, with the requisition only of one godfather. The rite to adults was publicly administered at Whitsuntide and Easter, by three immersions, and succeeded by confirmation. Prayers for the departed, that they might receive mercy, as a testimonial of belief in immortality, led gradually into doctrinal errors, and finally into the notion of purgatory.

Many Christians were in the army, in the state, and in civil service of various kinds, not even excepting the highest, as we see from the martyrdom of Apollonius' the senator, in the reign of Commodus, 184. The flourishing state of the Church was, however, grievously interrupted by the persecution of Severus, resulting in an edict of confiscation and death. The Church of Alexandria suffered beyond others; Leonides, the father of Origen, was among the first martyrs. Origen at his death, supported his family, having succeeded, although only eighteen years old, Clemens of Alexandria as master of the school of that place. Mammœa, the mother of Alexander Severus, sent for him to Antioch to hear him preach; and a prince of Arabia desired his presence at his court, to impart instruction in the Christian faith: so great was the fame of this excellent writer whose works, however, were considered unsound. He wrote the Octopla, being eight versions of the Septuagint in Greek and Hebrew, in parallel columns.

A.D. 210. One year before the death of Severus, Minicius Felix wrote his celebrated defence of Chris-

H

tianity, which was of great service to the Christian
church; to which also the rapid succession of emperors
was favourable. The Emperor Alexander Severus, the
fourth in succession to Severus in the space of twelve
years, favoured the Christians so far as to encourage them
to build temples for public worship, as appears from the
account handed over to us, in the matter of a dispute
between some tavern keepers and Christians about a
plot of land, which the Emporor decided in favour of the
latter, as most likely to make the fittest use of it. In
this reign, the Council of Iconium was called to decide
upon the validity of baptism administered by heretics and
Montanists. A succession of several emperors in a few
years was again favourable to church interests, which were
more endangered from within than without. (A.D. 242).
A bishop of Bostra in Arabia, Beryllus by name, revived the errors which had formerly been started by
Praxeas and Noetus. Origen confuting the error,
Beryllus returned into the communion of the church.
The gradual admixture of the philosophy of the East
and Platonism, had prepared the way for teaching
ascetic doctrines and retirement; and the persecutions
(A.D. 249) in the reign of Decius, the thirtieth Emperor of Rome, caused one Paul of Thebes to flee into
the desert, and commence an example which was followed by many others. Those who had sacrificed or
made terms during that persecution, were afterwards
received back into communion with the church too
readily, by letters from martyrs, or on other grounds.
Two synods, one under Cyprian at Carthage, and one
under Cornelius at Rome, decided upon adopting more
strict rules. Novatian, a presbyter at Rome, vehe-
mently opposed the admission of the once lapsed; and

effectually to oppose Cornelius, got himself irregularly ordained bishop by three obscure bishops from Italy; Novatus, a disgraced presbyter of Carthage, supported him. They made a party sufficiently strong to have a council, the first at Carthage, summoned against them. An important discussion took place shortly after the persecution, in the time of Valerian, thirty-second Emperor of Rome, 254. Two bishops having been deprived of office for crimes proved against them, were reinstated in their charges in Spain, by Stephen, bishop of Rome, as the bishop of the most powerful city of the West. Cyprian, bishop of Carthage, in a council called upon appeal to him, refused to acknowledge the deposed bishops Basilides and Martial, and decided that their substitutes should be recognized. The Council at Carthage likewise decided, that it was not necessary to defer baptizing infants till the eighth day after birth. The Western Church was divided from the Asiatic and African Church by the latter denying the validity of baptism by heretics. Upon this, Stephen of Rome roughly refused communion with the Eastern Church. The dispute was not settled till the death of Stephen. Paul of Samosata asserted the first elements of what in modern times has been held by Unitarian heretics. A council at Antioch, five years after Paul was made bishop of that see, having separated without coming to any decision upon the subject of the bishop's doctrinal orthodoxy, was succeeded by another deposing him, and moreover appointed another bishop in his stead. The Emperor Aurelian, as stated above, finally, in 272, rejected Paul, which is a striking evidence that temporal authority in church matters was, in the primitive Church, greater far than in England at this time. Diocletian, who assumed the

purple in 284, publicly protected the Christian Church;
but soon after persecuted it with the most bitter hatred.
This emperor, in 286, associated with himself three
rulers; and in 298, published an order that all persons
in office should present themselves at heathen sacrifices. Thus commenced a persecution which, throughout the empire, except in Gaul and Britain, governed
by Constantius, raged with increasing fury, until Constantine succeeding, united the whole empire under
one rule. St Alban, the first British martyr, was tortured and beheaded at Verulam, his native place, about
the time of the abdication of Diocletian. The legend
of the fiery cross appearing to the army of Constantine on approaching Rome to engage the tyrant Max-
entius, is connected by Eusebius with the conversion
of Constantine. He subsequently removed the seat of
the empire to Byzantium. Six years after, the edict
of Constantine at Milan favouring the Christian Church
— into which however, he himself was not admitted
till his final illness, 337 A.D.,— arose a dispute which
has remained in one or another form of error until this
day. Alexander, bishop of Alexandria, was accused
by Arius, a presbyter, of Sabellianism, through envy
at not having obtained the bishopric. Arius, opposing the teaching of Alexander which was said to be
unorthodox, maintained the Son to be essentially distinct from the Father. Constantine the Emperor, although not in full communion with the Church, convened the Council of Nice, A.D. 325, at which the
Arian doctrine was condemned—Eusebius, the father
of ecclesiastical history, giving his assent in such terms
that historians have reasonably suspected his own orthodoxy

Bishops of Jerusalem.	Antioch.	Heresies.	Councils.
Flourished.	Flourished.	45-73.	
James 32	Evodius 43	Ebionites	Jerusalem ...46
Symeon 62	Ignatius 70	Cerinthus	
Justus 104	Heros 107		

Apologists.		Persecutions.	
			A.D.
Quadratus ....} 125		Under Nero 64-69	
Aristides ....}		„ Domitian 94	
J. Martyr 148		„ Trajan 107	
		„ Hadrian.......................... 118	
Melito 166		„ Severus 202	
		„ Maximinus...................... 235	
Athenagoras 167		„ Decius 249	
Miltiades		„ Valerian 257	
Apolinarius .... }168-9		„ Aurelian.......................... 272	
Theophilus of Antioch		„ Diocletian 303	
Tatian......................			

Alexandria.	Rome—Bishops of the Early Church.	Heretics, Heresies, &c.	Councils.
	Died.		
Mark	1. Linus 58-78	114-144	
Amanus	2. Anencletus...... 68-91	Basilides and	
Abilius	3. Clement 93-100	Saturninus	
Cerdo	4. Evarestus 100	Carpocrites	
Primus	5. Alexander......109-116	Valentinus	
Justus	6. Sixtus............116-126	Cerdon	
Eumenes	7. Telesphorus...128-137		
	8. Hyginus.........138-141		
Marcus	9. Pius................142-157		
Celadion	10. Anicetus........156-168	Montanus	
Agrippinus	11. Sotes 168-177		
Julianus	12. Eleutherus 173-192	{Praxeas and Artemon	
Demetrius	13. Victor.............190-196		
	14. Zepherinus 201-219		
	15. Callistus........218-224		
	16. Urbanus.........222-231		
Heraclas	17. Pontianus 230-235		
	18. Anterus 236-238	{Beryllus and Noetus	}Synod at Rome v. Novatian
	19. Fabianus 251	Schism of No-vatus	
Dionysius	20. Cornelius 251-253		
	21. Lucius 252-255		
	22. Stephen 253-257	SabellianHeresy	{S. at Carthage on Bap. of Heretics
	23. Sextus.............257-259		
	24. Dionysius 259-271	Paul of Samosata	
Maximus	25. Felix 269-274-5	Manes	{S. at Antioch v. Paul of Samosata
Theanas	26. Eutichianus ...274-283		
	27. Caius 283-296		
Peter	28. Marcellinus.....296-304	Meletian Schism	
	29. Marcellus 303-309		
Achillas	30. Eusebius 310-311	Donatist Schism	{Arles v. Dona-tists, 314
	31. Melchiades 314		
Alexander	32. Sylvester 314-335		Nice

What were Christians first called?

What apostle was persecuted by Domitian?

When did Timothy suffer death?

When did the Church gather the Scriptures?

Who succeeded St John as historian of the Church?

What was the first Church in point of rank?

How far had Christianity spread about the end of the first century?

What did Pliny write to Rome for?

When did Saturninus live?

What other heretics do you know by name in the early part of the second century?

Who rebuilt Jerusalem?

Who were allowed to remain there?

Was Hadrian favourable to Christians?

Who was Celsus?

Who was Valentinus?

What other heresies arose?

What good resulted from the evil of "heresy?"

When did the Paschal controversy arise? Relate the details.

When was the subject settled?

Who was Montanus? and Dionysius of Corinth?

On what mission was Irenæus sent? and what do we gather from it?

Who was Lucius; and for what is he remarkable?

How did Irenæus oppose Victor, bishop of Rome?

What does he assert on Episcopal power and mission?

Who was Theodotus; and what was his heresy?

Give some account of the Council at Antioch in 269?

What remarkable fact is connected with this Council in their decision against Paul of Samosata?

Who first systematized error on the Trinity?

Who answered it?

What was the Sabellian heresy?

Give some account in detail of rules and ceremonies of the Primitive Church at this time?

What proves Christians were in high places in the second century?

What persecution was connected with Origen?

Give some account of him, and of Minicius Felix?

What is related of Alexander Severus?

Wherefore was the council called at Iconium in his reign?

Who was Beryllus, Paul of Thebes, Novatian, and Novatus?

Relate an incident in which the bishop of Rome attempted to control with undue authority?

What did the Council of Carthage decide touching the baptism of infants?

On what point did the Eastern and Western Churches disagree?

Give some account of Diocletian's reign?

What was the story of the "fiery cross?"

Was Constantine admitted into the Church before his final illness?

Give the date?

Was Eusebius suspected of being unorthodox?

State the principal heresies of the first three centuries.

PART III.

FROM THE CONVERSION OF THE NORTHERN INVADERS OF THE ROMAN EMPIRE TO THE FIRST TRANSLATION OF THE OLD TESTAMENT IN LATIN—THE INTRODUCTION OF CHRISTIANITY INTO BRITAIN TO THE BEGINNING OF THE NINTH CENTURY.

Constantine was doubtless influenced to support Christianity from motives of superstition, and from the influence which it had, having spread with varied degrees of success over the Roman and Persian empires, among the Goths of Thrace and Mysia, the Parthians, Scythians, and Germans. The internal portion of Church government, in rites, ceremonies, elections of bishops, power of having property, &c., remained in the hands of the prelates, the external government in the hands

the emperor, even the final decision of religious controversies was to a certain degree in the hands of the
emperor, as it had been in the time of Aurelian, and
the power of convoking œcumenical councils.

After forty-six years of alternate banishment and
recall, St. Athanasius was restored to his bishopric of
Alexandria by Constantius, who was one of the sons
of Constantine, among whom, on the death of the latter,
the empire was divided. Constans and Constantine
shared the empire of the West, and the former threat-
ened Constantius (who had supported, as emperor of the
Eastern empire the doctrine of Arius) with invasion if
he resisted the restoration of Athanasius. The last ves-
tiges of Paganism rapidly departed when Theodosius, surnamed the Great, in 388, called upon the senate of Rome
to make their election between Christianity and heathenism. Upon the decision in favour of the former, the vitality of Paganism for ever fled. The Suevi in Spain,
Vandals in Africa, the Ostrogoths in Pannonia, and other
northern hordes, as they gradually conquered the Roman
empire between the 5th and 6th centuries, successively
adopted the religion of the conquered. In 493, Clovis,
King of the Franks, was baptised, and so far was a
Christian: he rejected the universal heresy of Arius
which was embraced by all the barbarian conquerors in
the West. About thirty-four years after this event, Justinian began to reign, who, with the name of " the most
Christian: emperor," conferred upon him by the fifth
Council of Constantinople, yet died embracing the
heresy of the Phantastics, on the question which then
divided the Eastern church, as to whether the body of
Christ on earth was corruptible or incorruptible. The
emperor embraced the latter view. Ambrose, bishop of

Milan, when raised to that episcopate, was unbaptised; and it is a most remarkable evidence of the power which the Christian religion now exercised upon despotism, that he (A.D. 390) alone was able to impose upon Theodosius, called the Great, only eighty years after the Decian persecution, a penance for the bloody massacre of some obscure people at Thessalonica.

The year 345 is remarkable for the birth of Jerome, born at Stridona, on the confines of Dalmatia, A.D. 390. The translation of the Scriptures which he put forth was regarded by Rome as a dangerous innovation upon the custom of receiving the Septuagint. Nor was it till nearly two hundred years afterwards, that any distribution took place of that version which was ultimately to be received by the Western Church.

We now come to a period of ecclesiastical history which involves that of our own country. It was not much more than fifty years after the completion of St Jerome's great work, that Christianity suffered greatly in Britain by the invasion of the Saxons: it almost reproduced heathenism; however, the remoter places suffered least. It is worthy of remark, that Ireland and Scotland had been ever less under the influence of the Roman See than England. In the former country, the worship of God had been celebrated in the language of the country, and they had always refused obedience to the missives of Rome. The Church in Scotland, as we learn from Bede, manifested such aversion to those who came from Rome, that Daganus, a Scotch bishop, refused even to eat with them, so prevalent was the feeling of suspicion that temporal power, as well as Christianity, was at the bottom of every mission from Rome. The Saxon conquerors had, on payment

tribute, allowed the British Christians, who had fled to
Cornwall and Wales, to continue their worship, and
thirty-six years after the coming of Austin to Britain,
Bede tells us that they regarded that presbyter's proud
threats against their Church with contempt, and the
Roman mission with disgust. They followed the
Eastern Church in some rites and ceremonies, and in
the keeping of Easter. According to Bede, about 565,
thirty years before the appearance of Austin, St Columba came from Ireland, and converted the Picts; the
South Picts had, some years before, been converted by
Nynian, a British bishop. At the advent of Roman ecclesiastical power, the archbishop of Caerleon or St David's
exercised supreme authority. In the islands of Iona and
Anglesea, throughout Wales and Cornwall, Ireland and
Scotland, the Church, though weakened by the invasion
of the northern Saxons, was yet existing, but not
energetic, and only ten years before the mission of
Austin, Theonas bishop of London, and Thadioc archbishop of York, had retired into Wales, but not all the
clergy. Bertha, the Queen of Kent was a Christian, but
her chaplain, Lendhard, a native of France like his
mistress, refused the obedience due to Caerleon, and
wrote to Rome. Doubtless he wrote under the im-
pression of the truth of those subtle invasions upon the
Gospel, which taught that Christianity was only capable
of existing in union with Papacy. Nor can we blame
him for asserting what he believed to be founded upon
truth, and under the influence of which teaching he
had been ever brought up. It is remarkable, that at
the very period when Theonas and Thadioc retreated
with their flocks before the devastation of the Saxon
pagans, St Columba, from the lonely island of Icolmkill

(Iona), taught the Picts Christianity. He founded a school and monastery at Iona similar to that in which he had been brought up at Durrogh, in Ireland, founded by St Patrick, a pupil of St Germaine. St Germaine was bishop of Auxerre, in France, and had been sent to Britain at the request of the British prelates, to defend the orthodox views which were attacked by Pelagius, a native of Wales, who was finally condemned at a Council at Verulam, in 429 A.D.

The ancient British and Saxon churches gradually became united; and whether the succession of bishops be traced through St Augustine, who received his orders from the Roman Catholic Church, or through the ancient British line, the fact of apostolic succession is undeniable. And so the Church of England at no period ceased in the continuity of its bishops in lineal succession from the first founder down to the present bishops and archbishops. If it be asked, "But where were the bishops at the Reformation?" Why, as a body, they agreed and remained after the Reformation as before. Although forcibly expelled in the time of Mary, yet a sufficient number returned or survived till the accession of Elizabeth. Thus was a Divine Providence, we may trust, ever protecting the Anglican Church. In the time of the Commonwealth, the connection of the Church with the King was at least acknowledged. The Church, therefore, is identical, by lineal continuity, with that at the beginning of the Christian era; and by the bishops thereof, the ministers of the Church have been regularly ordained. Nay, the ancient sees founded by St Augustine, St Chad, St Swithin, and others, have for the most part remained the same. The ecclesiastical boundaries of our parishes are in many cases the same as those which existed in the time of our forefathers. The inhabitants, *at all times*, have been admitted by baptism into the visible church, received communion, professed their faith in the Trinity, and have used the same form in many points that the early Churches adopted from time immemorial. The very edifices and cathedrals have, in like manner, retained their substantial forms, rites, rights, and objects.

The events of the fourth century chiefly turned upon the destruction of the ancient heathendom of the nations of Greece and Rome. The fifth and sixth were marked by the opposing barrier set up by the Church against the ruthless Celtic invasions. Against them, the principle of " unity " of the Church took the important part of cementing otherwise heterogeneous views and peoples, although doubtless also preparing the way for Papal despotism, yet humanly speaking this sad error was not without its use among the lawless people of those ages.

Pelagius, the first bishop of Rome who had ever revolted against the custom of waiting for the consent of the king as essential to the appointment, had first argued the infallibility of the Roman bishop, and refused to communicate with the bishop of Constantinople till he renounced the title of Œcumenic or Universal Bishop. Gregory, called the Great, who succeeded Pelagius, first claimed for the bishop of Rome what was called the power of the keys, perhaps as a counterfoil to the title of Œcumenic, conferred by the Emperor Maurice on the patriarch of Constantinople. From the period of his death (A.D. 604) may be dated a continuous, though interrupted, manifestation of temporal power by the bishop of Rome. Rome had, since the barbarian conquest, changed her pretensions of

superiority founded upon local rank to others of a
spiritual nature—a clever plan, much more likely to impose upon barbarians converted to Christianity than
the assumption of any other kind of dignity founded
upon traditions they had destroyed. When Charlemagne was proclaimed Emperor of the West, the kingly
power of this great and pious man was exercised for
the welfare of the Church at large. The temporalities
he bestowed upon the Church conveyed great power to
Rome, and so enabled her to confine the notion of "Christianity" so that adherence to the injunctions of that see
was in fact regarded as a proof of it beyond all other.
Pepin dethroned Childeric III., King of France, by
means of the countenance of Zachary, the bishop of
Rome, who asserted, under pretence of Divine sanction,
that Pepin might rebel against his master. Sorely
pressed on all sides by the Lombards and the Greeks,
the former of whom had taken those provinces of Italy
which had remained longest attached to the Greek empire under the name of the Exarchate of Ravenna,
Zachary hoped by this perversion of Scripture to base
purposes to build the foundations of Rome's temporal
property. Stephen II., successor to Zachary, applied
for and obtained an army from Pepin, who conquered
the provinces, and (754-5) bestowed them upon the
Papal See. In 774 Charlemagne confirmed the gift
of Pepin, his father, and so obtained the credited, however fanciful, spiritual blessings of Rome, by which he
declared himself Emperor of the West (A.D. 800)—a
memorable period for the Church of Rome, as Charlemagne, by his munificence, greatly increased its despotic
power. Yet so greatly had the clerical character been de-
based, from serfs having orders conferred upon them, that

it was found necessary to reform the Church, and accordingly the councils of Aix la Chapelle and Frankfort (794) were called. While the Episcopal order was thus enlarged, Adrian I., the Pope, adopted other means of aggrandizing his own peculiar interests by the publication of the " False Decretals," and the " Donation of Constantine," two instruments received as genuine towards the end of the 8th century. They professed to be epistles and decrees of early Popes, and continued for six hundred years to remain among the bulwarks of the Papal See. All epistles of the early Church were called decretals; but it was not till about the year 494 that Pope Gelasius, in a synod at Rome, obtained for the papal decrees, equal and even superior authority to the canons of councils.

The seventh century was marked by the rise of Mahomet. This conquering religion, if so it may be called, spread from the north of the Euxine to the neighbourhood of the capital of the East; from Egypt to the northern shores of Africa, and from thence to Europe. Having overthrown the Gothic monarchy in 711, with Spain as a base of operations, the Moors crossed the Pyrénees, and overran the south-west provinces of France. In less than one hundred years, Europe, Asia, and Africa, had yielded more or less to Mohammedan prowess. After their defeat by Charles Martel, Duke of the Franks, at Tours (732), their power faded away in Europe.

There can be no question that religion in and after the time of Bonifice IV., who died in the early part of the seventh century, was sadly degraded from its original aggressive opposition to heathenism. And as if it were necessary to exert some unexpected pressure upon the Church at large to see to this, Mahomet arose as a scourge of Christendom, but nevertheless as a means indirectly of strengthening Christianity in the West. Conformity with Rome was now called "Unity of the Church:" it was so far useful as to present a kind of moral barrier to the headlong career of Mohammedanism. Mahomet had seen and marked but too well the length to which disputes among Christians could arrive; nor had he overlooked the gross superstitions which, as taught by the monks, actually prepared the way for his designs.

Among the chief of his advisers were Sergius, a Nestorian monk and excommunicated heretic, John of Antioch an Arian, Abdiah a Jew, and others. The Asiatic customs, which had prevailed in the British Islands and France, were gradually superseded by the pertinacity of Rome in demanding submission to her authority and customs. Perhaps all this had its influence in opposing Mohammedanism to an extent greater than we are apt to allow.

QUESTIONS.

To what countries had Christianity spread when Constantine became emperor?

What was the system of Church government?

In what way was Athanasius restored?

What decisive act accelerated the overthrow of Paganism?

What title did Justinian add to that of emperor?

Who were the Phantastics, and how was Justinian connected with their history?

What is remarkable respecting St Ambrose, and what striking evidence did he give of the power and stability of the Christian religion?

When was St Jerome born?

What great work did he undertake?

How long after that version did the Christian religion remain in Britain?

What is noted respecting the ritual of the Church in Ireland and Scotland, at the time of the Saxon invasion of England?

Who was Daganus?

How had the heathen Saxons treated the British bishops?

Who was St Columba?

Who was metropolitan of the Church at the time of St Austin's mission to the Saxons?

Where had the early British Church taken refuge?

Who were the bishops of York and London ten years before St Austin's mission?

Give some account of St Germaine and his students?

When gradually the powerful influence of Rome caused a fusion in the British and Saxon Churches, what results were worked out touching the Apostolic succession?

Have any ancient sees and cathedrals remained the same to this day?

What are the characteristics of the fourth and two following centuries?

Was the erroneous teaching of the Roman Church, on the subject of its power, productive of any good?

What did Pope Gregory claim for the Papacy; and why?

What did Pelagius also claim?

What king first increased the Roman temporal power?

What pope sanctioned the acts of Pepin?

What did Charlemagne add?

PART IV.

THE INNOVATION IN THE DOCTRINE OF THE HOLY EUCHARIST PREACHED BY PASCHATUS RADBERTUS— THE END OF THE FIRST TEN CENTURIES—THE CRU- SADES — THE DECLINE OF PAPAL POWER.

1087–1305.

In every age, the greatest reverence and the highest devotional respect has been used in the terms applied to the holy eucharist. But not until the 9th century did nice distinctions and subtle dogmas obtain any comparative power, nor were the figurative expressions and sacrificial terms selected for the communion service applied till then to the corporal presence of Christ, said to be in the bread and wine. The doctrine, that the words of consecration (differing at various periods) called forth the body of Christ from the invisible world to be transubstantiated in the eucharistic sacrifice, was first inculcated by Paschatus Radbertus about the year 831, only to be violently opposed by two learned men, Scotus and Bertram. Gross darkness and total absence of the spirit of the Holy Scriptures, characterize this age of the Church. It is remarkable, that about the 7th and 8th centuries, the true life of religion lost its vigour in France and Italy and increased in Britain. During the succeeding age it revived, under Charles the Great of France, and subsequently, amid almost universal loss of spiritual purity, it revived in Germany. Among the great controversies which had disturbed the peace of Rome, was that about image worship, carried on by Photius against the Roman See. In the year 853, Photius was raised to the patriarchate of the East by the Emperor Michael, who banished at the same time Ignatius, the actual bishop. Pope Nicholas I. eagerly espoused the cause of the deposed bishop, by assembling a council and restoring him, as far as excommunication and documents in his favour could do so. The matchless impertinence of acting always upon the principle of assuming power without reality, was the usual method of Rome, whose bishop was excommunicated by Photius in a council at Constantinople. Meanwhile Bulgaria, which had been converted by Greek missions, was added to

I

the patriarchate, together with a few provinces east of the Adriatic. Rome had in some sort regarded these as under her protection, consequently this only served to increase mutual hatred. Both bishops were influenced very little by Christianity, and their disputes ended at last in the separation of the Churches of the East and West. And although some shadow of reverence has been the pretext for Rome to acknowledge a degree of union, disobedience to the temporal authority of the Roman episcopate has never been forgiven or forgotten.

It is curious to remark, that one of the five marks of heresy urged by Photius as the grounds of excommunicating the bishop of Rome, was, that of "forbidding to marry" in the priesthood. The other great disputes were the doctrine of salvation by *grace*, and the doctrine of transubstantiation. Lethargy of all intellect caused the gradual dying out of controversy till the 11th century, when Berenger (1045), bishop, or as some say archdeacon, of Angers in France, was said to have promulgated opinions opposed to the doctrine first taught by Radbertus 200 years before, even after a formal sentence of deprivation of his temporalities had been pronounced by Henry I. Hildebrand, who was his friend, caused Berenger to sign a confession of the real presence without any change of substance, in that way narrowly (1078) escaping (such was the violence of several ecclesiastics) the fiery ordeal. He frequently signed, and as often retracted confession of the doctrine of transubstantiation. Thus whilst we admire his learning, and venerate the cause for which he displayed his talents, his tergiversation proved that a character of far sterner sort was wanted to be the champion against the errors he opposed so feebly.

It was not till the 13th century that the custom of elevating the eucharist after consecration began. Then also arose the teaching, that the angelic salutation to the Virgin, repeated one hundred and fifty times, was equal in efficacy to the Lord's Prayer repeated fifteen times. Dominic, afterwards canonized, reckoned these prayers by beads, and the whole ceremony obtained the name of "Rosary." The Carmelites represented the scapulary, a portion of the monk's dress, as conveying holiness and mystic influence. In fact, there was no end to the various alterations and additions to worship in this century, shewing the very great need of a general and complete reformation.

1095. In the latter part of the 11th century, only seven years after the death of Berenger one of the first pioneers of the Reformation, at a council which met at Clermont in Auvergne, Pope Urban originated the crusades, chiefly through the representation of Peter the Hermit. The words of Urban were—"Si quisquam in viâ, sive in pugnâ, pro Christo moreretur, in numero martyrum absolutus ab omnibus peccatis suis computaretur." If any one should, while engaged in the crusade or in battle, die for Christ, he should be numbered among the martyrs, and be absolved from all sins.

But the first public appeal to the Universal Church, exhorting to the rescue of Jerusalem from the infidels, was made by Sylvester, the second of that name. It was owing to the plenary indulgences first granted to the crusaders, and afterwards to others, that the ruin of the penitential system, which, when exercised according to the ancient canons, had been useful and salutary, was completed.

Doubtless the Christians, from the 7th century, had suffered, though not so grievously as might have been imagined, from the dominion of the Mohammedan, but in the 11th century the Turkish dynasty succeeded the Mohammedan Cailiphs of Bagdad, and treated them very differently. Pilgrims carried the tale of suffering to all parts of Europe; and Rome, too glad to obtain power over those large bodies of warlike spirits, which only served to sustain empires and kings in opposition to her, readily supported a systemized invasion of a far and foreign land. Multitudes passed into Asia Minor, and formed even principalities in the heart of the Greek empire. Four years after Pope Urban's spirited exhortation, which is still extant, the first Christian army, led by Godfrey of Bouillon, Duke of Lorrain, took Jerusalem, which remained a Latin kingdom for a period of eighty years, though the country around was in the possession of the Crescent.

The Crusaders forced, however, many of the Greek bishops to the allegiance of Rome, profaned their churches, and expelled their clergy. These proceedings sometimes rendered the Greeks as little desirous of the crusaders as those who were opposed to them, and caused still greater estrangement between the two Churches of the East and West. The feelings upon this point were well expressed by Nechites, archbishop of Nicomedia, in his conference with a Latin bishop in 1137: "We do not refuse," said he, "among her sisters, the first rank to be assigned to Rome; and we acknowledge that she presides at a general council, but she is separated from us by her pride when, exceeding her power, she divided the empire and the Churches of the East and West. We should only be slaves, not children of the Church, when Rome would alone enjoy liberty and give laws to all others, without being subject to any herself. We do not find in any creed, that we are bound to confess the Roman Church in particular, but one Holy Catholic and Apostolic Church. This is what I say of the Roman Church, which I revere with you; but I do not believe it a duty to follow her necessarily in all things, nor that we ought to relinquish our rites, and adopt her mode of administration of sacraments, without examining it by reason and by Scripture."

The Decretals of the Popes obtained, in the year 1151, increased weight and began to be multiplied in number, chiefly through the artifice of Gratian, a monk of Bologna. He published a book called " The Decrees," divided into three parts, called the Distinction, the Causes, the Consecration—treating respectively of canons, jurisdiction, and divine rites. This, and the collection made subsequently by Gregory the Ninth, became a kind of basis of all scholastic knowledge in the universities of Europe. Boniface VIII. added others in 1299, with the further addition in the succeeding age, of the " Clementines," which were again followed by the "Extravagants"—a name taken from a work on the same subject by Circa, bishop of Faenza, in 1191, and so called from their treating of matters not in the Decretals of 1151.

Edessa, a Christian principality since the first crusade, having been retaken by the Turks, Pope Eugenius proclaimed a second crusade. Lewis VII. of France, and the Emperor of Germany, led immense armies, in the vain hope of effectually assisting the Christians. Saladin, Sultan of Egypt and Syria, waged war with great success against the divided and factious Latins,

finally took Jerusalem, and put an end to their dominion. A pestilence destroyed a third army under
Barbarossa of Germany, who was drowned in a river of
Cilicia. Philip Augustus, King of France, and Richard
of England, headed another in the following year (1190):
But the Mohammedan power, in the face of great dis-
asters, remained established. In 1203–6 a crusade,
which only terminated in a cruel oppression of the
Greek Church and empire, was finally put an end to by
the Greek Emperor and Patriarch expelling the Latin
invaders from Constantinople, which they had taken.
Six different and fruitless expeditions, from the year
1217–40, saw Jerusalem recovered and retaken, till
the last remnant of the Christian power fell at the siege
and capture of Acre in 1291. The crusades increased
the power of Rome, by placing in the hands of the
popes much arbitrative power, in consequence of temporal as well as spiritual property being intrusted to
their charge. The idea of papal power securing remission of sins gained further ground from the preaching,
that "holy expeditions were able to wipe off and blot out
any amount of sins;" and as that remission came by way
of Rome only, her power was enormous and unprece-
dented, above all canon law and every national and con-
stitutional law. The various religious orders were her
great supporters, because they were not subject to the
proper jurisdiction of their bishops, but to the Pope only.
They became audacious and luxurious—far different
from what the ancient monastic vows and examples
required; for the sole universal rule of the ancient
ascetics was that they should "live in monastries, should
work in silence, and eat their own bread!"

Yet did corruption work silently, but no less surely,

upon the vitality of this seeming greatness. Kings
and pontiffs were equally unaware of the impercep-
tible change gradually working its way. One instance
is worth relating here. A fund, purposing to be
applied to the crusades, was spent in supporting the
King of France in his usurpation of the kingdom
of Arragon. This fund was granted to the French
monarch with surpassing effrontery by the Pope, in the
face of the claimants in the family of Peter of Arragon — who however were, in spite of excommunication, restored in the person of the son of Peter, by a
treaty with Charles the Second of Anjou. Honorius,
the Pope, bitterly inveighed against Charles for refusing to support him in his iniquity. But the time had
come when kings no longer resigned their thrones at
the bidding of Rome, for power assumed and ex-
erted in vain is necessarily weakened. Among other
ill-timed assertions of the papal right of interference
in State affairs, Pope Nicholas absolved Charles from
his oath to the house of Arragon. This only served
to increase hatred and silent opposition from kings and
people, till Boniface VIII. (Benedict Cajetan) roused
their indignation to the highest by his bull, " Unam
Sanctam," which declared all temporal power to be
vested in himself. His death in 1305 hastened,
doubtless, the gradually decreasing prestige of the
temporal power of the Roman See, which may be said
to have reached its culminating point in the time of
Hildebrand, in the latter part of the 11th century.

. As the abuses of the Church had been more than
ordinarily rife in Germany, so it was there that the
people had been gradually endeavouring to obtain concordats similar to those which, in France, from the time

of Louis IX., had existed by the Pragmatic Sanction.
The emperors and the popes had ever been at variance;
battles and miseries throughout four centuries had prepared the people to receive with intense satisfaction, any
system opposed to that which had been connected with
all their troubles. (1414.) The concordats of Constance
and Aschaffenburg had been almost totally ignored by
the papal court—a line of conduct which nourished
feelings of the bitterest animosity, which burst forth
into action when the man and the hour came.

While many holy men, cardinals, popes, and others,
ordered their life and conversation by the religion of
Christ, yet they were but a very imperfect counter-
balance to the vast mass of haughtiness, luxury, and
immorality in high places. No spiritual power exercised so outrageously could long hold its own even
among the superstitious and ignorant. When that
depravity had descended, and the zeal and piety of
the inferior clergy began to be poisoned by pernicious
example, the Church of Rome reeled to its foundation; so that the saying of Pius II., in reference to the
profligacy of the clergy, " that if there were good reasons for enacting the law of celibacy, there were greater
for its removal altogether," became too true to be denied
by the most zealous upholders of papal purity.

We now shall consider the attempts at reformation
made by the Church of Rome within herself. The
first attempt with any real intention was, when the
Council of Pisa was convened by the cardinals to settle
the schism caused by the rival popes, Gregory XII.
and Benedict XIII., in March 1409.

Did the primitive Church define the doctrine of the real presence?

Who first published erroneous doctrines of the Holy Sacrament?

Who opposed the author?

When did he flourish?

Who supported him?

Who was Photius?

Relate some of the incidents of his time?

What mark of heresy did Photius mention among others?

Who was Berenger?

In what did he fail as a reformer?

When was the elevation of the host first commenced?

What is "The Rosary?"

When was the first crusade originated?

By whom, and at whose instigation?

What were the words by which the Pope endeavoured to enlist soldiers in the cause?

When was the first public appeal made?

What first lessened the power of the ancient canons?

Why had Rome been induced to interest herself in the crusades?

Who led the first Christian army against the Turks?

What was the result with reference to the Greek Church?

What did this cause? How were they expressed by a bishop of that Church?

What were the Decretals?

Give a short account of some of them?

What were the "Clementines" and "Extravagants?"

Who proclaimed the second crusade? Who led it?

Who led another in the year 1190?

What resulted from a crusade in the year 1203-6?

How many crusades took place between 1217-40?

How did they affect the Roman See?

Who were the great supporters of the papal power? and why?

What instance, amid the seeming greatness of Rome, was an evidence of the coming judgments?

What did the bull of Boniface VIII. assert?

When were abuses most palpable?

Why?

Why was France less exposed to them?

What rival popes ruled in the beginning of the 15th century?

PART V.

THE FIRST ATTEMPT AT REFORMATION DURING THE
COUNCILS OF CONSTANCE, BASLE, AND THE FIFTH
LATERAN.

Among so many of the wise and holy of the Roman
Church, it would have been strange indeed if no tentative efforts at reaching forward to a purer and more
perfect condition had never been entered upon. Thus,
the word reformation was not necessarily connected with
any taint of heresy. Synodical and other right methods
of correcting abuses and imperfections had been set on
foot by many bold and learned ecclesiastics (among
whom, first in rank, were the fathers of the church in
Council at Pisa, 1409), though not till the great schism
and subsequent residence of the popes at Avignon had
given to the world undoubted evidence of weakness and
vice, as the following words of the Cardinal of Cambrai
(1410) declared. The church, said d'Ailli, "has arrived
at such a pass, that it deserves only to be governed by
reprobates." Nicholas of Clemangis, who had been
secretary to Benedict III., in an address to the Council
of Constance, ascribed the schism to the frightful
wickedness of the rulers and pastors of the Church.
Among the Germans, the earliest treatise on the Reformation of the Church was written by Henry de Langenstein of Hesse; in the five last chapters of which
work, he describes the universal profligacy of the
clergy. The pontificate of Benedict IX., a shameful
period in the annals of the Roman See, was marked by

the appearance from England of a remonstrance entitled the " Golden Mirror of the Pope."

The Italians profiting most, were least averse to that general corruption, which even excited the Spaniards to vent in satire what was not safely to be expressed otherwise. The Council of Pisa was the first which met ostensibly for the purpose of reform. They endeavoured to cut short the schism of the popes by declaring the papal seat vacant, and proceeding to the election of Alexander V. The period was so far favourable to their designs that certain concessions were obtained from that pope, which, though in reality amounting to very little, yet seemed to proclaim an important fact, that general councils were supreme. The next council was held at Constance, in a land more favourable to the development of right principles than the slavish cities of Italy. Gerson, chancellor of the University of Paris, led the assault, by attacking the Decretals, the Clementines, and most of the Constitutions of the pope. A council of reform, which numbered three cardinals among its members, began its deliberation in August 1415. Robert Hallam, bishop of Salisbury, was an active reformer, and exercised considerable influence not only in the council, but over the mind of the Emperor Sigismund, who vainly opposed the election of a pope, but at last yielded assent to the election of Martin V. The Italian clergy, though luxurious and base, were a model of behaviour compared with the papal court or the clergy of the German empire. Consequently the nineteen articles, determined upon in the reform committee, were coldly supported by the Transalpine clergy, who could not see any necessity for reform.

With regard to the secular clergy, simony and concubinage were the chief offences aimed at. Regulations for the purification of the several orders, the mendicants particularly, were also devised by the reformers of the Council of Constance. At the fortieth session, the nineteen points above alluded to were submitted to the new pope, Martin V. The French and Germans were getting wearied with the unfaithful prolongation of the committee, accordingly Sigismund reminded some deputies on the occasion, that as they had not supported him in desiring to bind the unelected pope to agreements, now they had elected one without, they must abide the consequences which he had in a measure foretold them. The Council of Constance did what Pisa had begun, by not only asserting that a general council was superior to the individual authority of a pope, but proceeded to withdraw allegiance from the last of the three popes, Benedict, who clung with the avarice of age to his papal throne. Angelo Corrasio, Gregory XII., Peter de Luna, Benedict XIII., and John XXIII., were the three rival popes, the first of which sunk into obscurity; the second fought till he was obliged to resign; and John was degraded. The schism was finally ended by the election of Martin V. (1417) to a throne which had been held by two pretenders and a profligate. The Council shortly after adjourned for the space of five years. Peter de Luna continued for six years to thunder his anathemas from his retirement; and at his death (1424), not unsuspected of being tortured by poison, he commanded his two faithful cardinals, who had retired to Paniscola with him, to elect a successor, Baltaza Cossa. John XXIII. retired as a simple ecclesiastic to Parma, where he found many to sympathize with, and even to express a desire to restore him. He however, suddenly presented himself at the feet of Martin, and acknowledged him as the true pope ;. and the conduct of these two bishops exhibits certainly a magnanimity too rare in the papal annals to be left unnoticed. John XXIII., wholly unqualified as he was for the lowest ministry in God's Church, a mere soldier, with a code of morality too like that which was observed by military men, yet attracted many friends by a manly and candid disposition.

The clamour for reformation was increased by many individual champions of the Church itself, among others,| Pierri d'Ailli, cardinal of Cambrai, and John Gerson, and the Florentine Savanarola. France had the honour of the most distinguished; Germany of the greatest number. Savanarola was born at Ferrara in 1452; but Florence was the sphere of his great mission.

Although the papal power had become so hateful to the Christian world, yet the reforming councils were nevertheless possessed of the loftiest and most bigoted views of the authority of the Church of Rome. For, while the Council of Constance deposed a legitimate pope on the one hand, they burned Huss and Hussites on the other; and persecuted heresy so called with unmitigated ferocity. Martin, by dissolving the Council of Constance, succeeded in checking the dangerous spirit, which was a triumph of no small importance.

· In the thirty-ninth session, however, a decree had been enacted, that general councils should be held every ten years, in addition to *two* within the first ten years. Basle at length met after two pretended and scantily attended councils; a month before which however, Martin died (1431). The incapacity of Eugenius IV the successor of Martin, and his absurd opposition to the reforms intended by the Cardinals and Fathers at Basle, ended in his being formally suspended from his dignity. Attacked by the Duke of Milan abroad, and opposed by his subjects who were universally discontented, the Emperor Sigismund, moreover, declaring on the side of the Cardinals, Eugenius suddenly lowered his pretensions, withdrew his offensive edicts against the Council, and with a cunning which was a too common instrument of the Papal Court, sent two legates to Basle with the design of embarrassing the Council, in which designs they had but too well succeeded.

A final breach between the Council and the Pope succeeded upon the latter haughtily proceeding to transfer the Council to Ferrara. From that time, if not from the beginning, the legitimacy of this Council (Basle) has been always disputed by the Roman writers, who, however, allow its proceedings to be binding upon the Church up to the period of the publication in 1439 of the "Eight Propositions" against Pope Eugenius. Felix V., Amadeus, Duke of Saxony, elected to the papal throne, created a kind of second great schism; for, on the Council being dissolved, and removing itself to Lyons or Lausanne, the rival session of disputants, who supported Eugenius in spite of his deposition, remained at Florence, but subsequently withdrew to Rome. Felix V., the creature of the Council of Basle, resigned, upon the election of Nicholas V. in the place of Eugenius IV. This happy escape from a second schism, and worse political dilemma, quite overwhelmed the thoughts of persecution; even the Hussites were forgotten in the general joy, which was celebrated in the commemorative verse:

"Fulsit lux mundo; cessit Felix Nicolao."

The French held a Council at Bourges contemporary with the session of the Council of Basle. The result of these labours was a Pragmatic Sanction, which protected the Gallican kingdom from any exercise of papal authority in temporals, and also controlled the acknowledged supreme authority in spirituals by canons and regulations of the *ancient councils* of the Church. This continued, with the exception of the attempt of Louis XI. to resign the freedom the Pragmatic Sanction gave, until the time of Francis I. Thus France, which never beheld the worst side of the papal extortion and despotism, was far from desiring that complete change of the Roman system and doctrine under which Germany had for so many years suffered and groaned in vain. And, accordingly, from Germany proceeded the scourge which was ultimately to shake the Roman See to the foundation.

Long before the time of Luther, the universities of Germany were, in some measure, the fountains of all learning as far as it went. But when the scholastic theory came under the influence of a newer and freer system supported by a party formidable rather by their unity than their number, it gradually became undermined. It was as much by the disputes of the younger reformers in learning as by the matter of the indulgences, that the first steps to the Reformation were laid (A.D. 1514). Reuchlin, a lawyer, exposed in strictly formal legal phrase the ignorance of some scholastic libels upon certain Hebrew works. Vindictive and determined, the Dominicans, to whose hands the professional seats were chiefly intrusted, returned the compliment, by declaring the answer of Reuchlin heretical—not in any Protestant sense, however; questioning any Romish ʳ trine never entered the head of that learned writer. On the contrary, both Dominicans, inquisition, and university on the one side, and Reuchlin on the other, appealed to the Bishop of Rome. Thus were these leaders, as it were, forced into parties, which declared for liberty of opinion and opposed Roman supremacy. The merits of the case were not even considered, but all merged into what was felt by the emperor, and those cities which supported Reuchlin, to be the real question, namely, whether piety or unrestricted zeal for the Church without it, was most worthy of being called Christianity, whether mental cultivation or crassid ignorance were to advance, whether the study of the classics, or the books of Remigius and Cornutus, and the "Summa" of Thomas Aquinas, should prevail in the universities. Thus did these quarrels of the early part of the 16th century open to the young mind of many a scholar the rich treasures of forgotten learning, as well as sanction the idea of disputation upon subjects heretofore closed to discussion by the seal of the Roman Papacy.

We cannot so well, on the whole, illustrate the nature of affairs as regards the attempted reformation of the Church from within, than by quoting some portions of the epistles which were addressed to the Council of Basle by Cardinal Julian Cesarini, called by Bossuet the greatest man of his age. He had been placed in the office of president of that council by Martin, and had been continued in it by Eugenius, as a zealous friend of the Church.

"One great motive with me to join this council, was the deformity and dissoluteness of the German clergy, on account of which the laity are immoderately irritated against the ecclesiastical state ; so much so, as to make it matter of serious apprehension whether, if they be not

reformed, the people will not rush, after the example of
the Hussites, upon the whole clergy, as they publicly
menace to do. Moreover, this deformity gives great
audacity to the Bohemians, and great colouring to the
errors of those who are loudest in their invectives
against the baseness of the clergy; on which account,
had a general council not been convoked at this place,
it had been necessary to collect a provincial synod for
the reform of the German clergy; since, in truth, if
that clergy be not corrected, even though the heresy of
Bohemia should be extinguished, others would rise up
in its place." . . . "If you should dissolve this
council, what will the whole world say, when it shall
learn the act? Will it not decide that the clergy is
incorrigible, and desirous for ever to grovel in the filth
of its own deformity? Many councils have been celebrated in our days, from which no reform has proceeded;
the nations are expecting that some fruit should come
from this. But if it is dissolved, all will exclaim that
we laugh at God and man. As no hope of our correc-
tion will any longer be left, the laity will rush, like
Hussites, upon us. This design is already publicly
rumoured. The minds of men are pregnant; they are
already beginning to vomit the poison intended for our
destruction. They will suppose that they are offering
a sacrifice to God, when they shall murder or despoil
the clergy. Sunk in general estimation into the depth
of evil, these last will become odious to God and the
world, and the very moderate respect which is now felt
for them will entirely perish. This council is still some
little restraint upon secular men; but as soon as they
shall find their last hope fail them, they will let loose
the reins of public persecution." . . . "Should the

K

council be dissolved, the people of Germany, seeing themselves not only deserted but deluded by the Church, will join with the heretics, and hate us even more than they. Alas! how frightful will be the confusion! how certain the termination!" . . . Already I behold the axe laid at the root. The tree is bending to its fall, and can resist no longer. And certainly, though it could stand of itself, we ourselves should precipitate it to earth. . . . "Again, should a prorogation be proposed and a transfer of place, to the end that in the presence of your holiness greater blessings may be accomplished, no man living will believe it. We have been deluded (they say) in the Council of Sienna: so it is again in this; legates have been sent out, bulls have been issued; nevertheless a change in the place is now sought, and a delay in the time. What better hope will there be then? Most blessed Father, believe me, the scandals which I have mentioned will not be removed by this delay. Let us ask the heretics, whether they will delay for a year and a-half the dissemination of their virulence? Let us ask those who are scandalized at the deformity of the clergy, if they will for so long delay their indignation? Not a day passes in which that heresy does not sprout forth; not a day in which they do not seduce or oppress some Catholics: they do not lose the smallest moment of time. There is not a day in which new scandals do not arise from the depravity of the clergy; yet all measures for their remedy are procrastinated! Let us do what can be done now. Let the rest be reserved for this year and a-half. For I have great fears that, before the end of the year and a-half, unless means be taken to prevent it, the greater part of the clergy of Germany will be in desolation. It is certain, that if the word should be once spread through Germany that the council is dissolved, the whole body of the clergy would be consigned to plunder." . . . "But I hear that some are apprehensive lest the temporalities should be taken away from the Church by this council. A strange notion! Though, if this council did not consist of ecclesiastics, there might be some question on the subject. But where shall we find the ecclesiastic who would consent to such a project? not only from its injustice, but from the loss the body would sustain from it. And where the layman? There are none or next to none! And if some princes should haply send their ambassadors, they will send, for the most part, ecclesiastics, who would in no wise consent. Even the few laymen who will be present, will not be admitted to vote on matters strictly ecclesiastical; and I scarcely think that there will be, upon the whole, ten secular lords present, and perhaps not half so many. But if we dismiss the council, the laity will come and take our temporalities indeed. When God wishes to inflict any misfortune upon any people, He first so disposes that their dangers shall not be perceived nor understood. And such is now the condition of ecclesiastics; they are not blind, but worse than blind; they see the flame before them, and rush headlong into it." . . . "Within these few last days I have received intelligence which should tend still further to divert you from dissolving the council. The prelates of France have assembled at Bourges, and, after long and scrupulous investigation, have decided that this council is not only legitimate, but must also of necessity be celebrated both in this place and at this time; and so the French clergy are about to join it. The reasons which have moved them to this were sent at the same time, and have been forwarded to your holiness. Why then do you longer delay. You have striven with all your power, by messages, letters, and various other expedients, to keep the clergy away; you have struggled with your whole force utterly to destroy this council. Nevertheless, as you see, it swells and increases day by day, and the more severe the prohibition, the more ardent is the opposite impulse. Tell me now—Is not this to resist the will of God? Why do you provoke the Church to indignation? Why do you irritate the Christian people? Condescend, I implore you, so to act, as to secure for yourself the love and goodwill, and not the hatred of mankind."

QUESTIONS.

What was the earliest Council of Reform in the Roman religion? Give its date.

What celebrated characters bore testimony to the corruption in the Church?

What did the Council of Pisa attempt?

Where was the next council held?

Who was Hallam?

What Reform Committee met, and what did they effect?

What was effected at the fortieth session?

Who were the rival popes in the great schism?

What ultimately became of them?

Who were Pietre d'Ailli, and John Gerson, and Savanarola?

Were the reformers of the Church averse to undue exertion of her power?

What proof did they give of their hatred of opposition?

What was enacted at the thirty-ninth session of the Council of Constance?

When did the Council of Basle meet?

How did Pope Eugenius act towards this council?

Why has this council been disputed by Romanists?

Was there any probability of a second schism?

Where did the French Church hold a council during the session of Basle, and with what results?

Who was willing to betray the freedom thereby gained to the Gallican Church?

Who was Reuchlin?

How did he become mixed up in controversy?

When did these disputes take place?

What did they cause?

Who was Julian Cesarini; and what was the general view he took of ecclesiastical affairs?

PART VI.

THE FIRST CHECKS OF THE CHURCH IN EUROPE, AND PARTICULARLY OF THE ANGLICAN BRANCH, TO PAPAL USURPATION—THE TIME OF WICKLIFFE—HIS OPINIONS INFUSED INTO BOHEMIA BY J. HUSS—PERSECUTION OF REFORMERS IN 1400.

As all spiritual power was centered in the court of Rome, so the desire for temporal power tempted the popes to interest themselves in the disputes of countries and kings. It may safely be said that the extravagant notions on this point held by Boniface VIII., was the turning point of the subsequent defeat of the Papacy. The fixed and distinctive principle on which the Gallican Church founded her liberties, was the inferiority of the Pope to a general council. The differences between Boniface and Philip the Fair of France, resulted in the calling by the former of a council at Rome (1302), to deliberate on the disputes. The wording of the bull, on this occasion, was so haughty and violent, that it was burnt by the equally haughty king; nevertheless, at that council was published the celebrated assertion of divine authority over every temporal power contained in the bull "Unam sanctam." Philip sent (1303) messengers to seize the Pope at Anagni near Rome, and take him prisoner. He died from rage and vexation; and the success of the French interest continued from that day in the court of Rome. One of the most important assertions against the Roman usurpation of power in England, was in the statute (A.D. 1275) of "Præmunire" against all clergy charged with felony, allowing the civil courts to try them. The statute was so called from the first two words, "Præmunire facias," or "cause X. Y. to appear" to free himself from charges, which, if proved, subjected the defendant to the loss of the king's protection in goods and lands; and imprisonment. Four years afterwards, by the law of "Mortmain," Edward I. made his consent necessary for the ratification of property bequeathed to the Church.

Ten years after the death of Wickliffe (1384), the penalties of præmunire were enforced against those who procured "bulls" from Rome. Whether this law, which was first passed in 1275, was put into action through the weakness of the papal authority by reason of the "*Great schism*" (1380), as it was called, we cannot now ascertain; but certain it is, that from that period may be dated the gradual independence of the Church of England as regards the papal control. Nor had the legitimate influence of the Church been usurped in other countries without a silent, but nevertheless lasting desire to take every opportunity of recovering what in ancient times had existed. The Council (1431) of Baale, which met pursuant to a decree of that of Constance, providing a general council to meet every ten years, whether the Pope summoned or not, abolished

the "annates" or the year's revenue of every vacant
bishopric claimed by the Pope, on pretence of defending
Christendom from the infidels; restored to Chapters the
elections hitherto claimed by the Pope to vacant bishop-
rics, as well as benefices to the local bishops, and declared that a general council was above the Pope. Eugenius IV. (1438) after summoning a council at Ferrara excommunicated the members of the Council of Basle, who,
in turn, elected Amadeus, Duke of Savoy, under the title
of Felix V., and deposed Eugenius.* Charles VII. of
France called a mingled council of one hundred and nine
nobility and bishops, who reduced the decrees of the
Council of Basle into an edict, called the Pragmatic
Sanction. This unpalatable state of things was gradually merged into the concordat which Leo X., frightened
at the spread of the Reformation, entered into with
Francis I. This defined and systemized on reasonable
grounds the authority of the Pope and the kings of
France, to the very sensible advantage of the latter.

This was the second concordat which France had
extorted on condition of supporting the Pontiff; for in
1268, Louis, the ninth of the line, had obtained another
Pragmatic sanction.

As oppressive extortions and contempt had been the
sole reward of England's general subjection to the Pope,
there only needed some channel for conveying the feelings of the people to let loose floods of pent-up anger.
When Cardinal Otho represented at Reading the necessities of the Pope caused by his conflict with the
Emperor Frederick of Germany, and demanded a fifth
of the clergy's (1240-44) property—when some time
after, a mandate came to the Archbishop of Canterbury

* See Part V.

and Bishops of Lincoln and Salisbury, to appoint three hundred Roman subjects to vacant benefices — when (A.D. 1245) Italians held benefices amounting in value to 60,000 marks of silver—vigorous efforts were made from time to time to signify to the Pope how these abuses wounded the feelings of the people and clergy at large.

Grostete, Bishop of Lincoln, was one of the honest friends of the Church of England. He opposed with firmness and meekness the Pope's shameless friars riding about the country collecting his taxes. He opposed the king equally and supported the Pope, when rectitude called upon him to do so. In 1256, when Pope Alexander IV. gave a deanery to one Geordano, an Italian, who was secretly installed by two other strangers sent by the Pope, Sewell, Archbishop of York, a friend of Grostete, was excommunicated for refusing to consider the appointment valid. He died in jail in excommunication, and was revered as a martyr by the people.

Richard, Bishop of Chester, another friend of Grostete, had sided with Grostete and the barons in refusing a tax of three years' tenths on benefices, for the purposes of a crusade. The barons were, however, ultimately overcome (1267) in battle. Perhaps as good an index to the general change of view commencing at this period, is the fact, that the building of monasteries began to be discontinued, and colleges were founded in large numbers at Cambridge and at Oxford.

Wickliffe was the means of expression only of sentiments long before ripening into maturity. The papal bull which thundered against the anti-papal opinions broached by him, was so little regarded at Oxford, where he occupied in 1377 the theological chair, that it narrowly escaped ignominious rejection. Certainly, considering the rash assertions of Wickliffe, and his views on transubstantiation, penance, auricular confession, and papal power, it is honourable to the age that he died for his rectory at Sutterworth.

His opinions were rather those which would be received as they were in an after age. His works were rare; at least on the Continent they were chiefly known through being distributed probably by Bohemians who had studied at Oxford; be that as it may, they fell into the hands of John Huss, who in 1400, was confessor to Sophia of Bavaria, Queen of Bohemia. Defending the rights of his university (Prague) against the Germans, who had obtained from their numbers a great preponderance in authority, he incurred their hatred and opposition. The cardinals, assembled at Pisa in opposition to Gregory XII., were supported by Huss, and thus excited the indignation of that prelate, who forthwith issued a prohibitory decree against Huss. After the extinction of the great schism, John XXIII. furnished Huss with another matter for reprehension, in desiring a crusade against Ladislaus, King of Naples; granting to those who would engage in it the usual indulgences. The people had now learned to condemn this mockery, and accordingly the pontifical missionaries were opposed, and even ran some danger in executing their office. Huss, who acknowledged without hesitation the authority, was summoned before the Council of Constance. However, he dispatched a letter to a friend immediately before his departure, which prophesied his fate. He was accused and condemned, in defiance of the express promise of personal safety guaranteed by the Pope, and this pure and perfect Christian and churchman was burnt to death (1416). "Such was the end," says Poggio the Florentine, "of a man incredibly excellent — the final catastrophe I beheld myself." The condition of Bohemia was especially flourishing at that time; but shortly after this execution, the nobles and people gave indications of a spirit which caused Martin V. to publish a bull of crusade against them as heretics, and the differences were henceforth fairly committed to the decision of the sword. It is impossible to trace even the names of parties thenceforward (1433–1466) opposing Roman influence; but by the compact of Iglau, the cup was conceded to the Bohemians, and two priests set in the churches to administer the sacrament in both kinds to those who wished it, and the sacrament in one kind to the rest. Yet even so late as 1467, according to Beausobre, a body of religionists, on separating from the Roman Church, made application to the Vaudois for apostolical succession, and one Matthew was consecrated bishop. Having partially disappeared, they suddenly, in the year 1504, arose into some notice under the name of United Brethren, as they called themselves; thus did Luther find ranged at his side a numerous body of hereditary reformers rejecting the six great errors of Rome.

At this time the conscience of the people was ruled by casuistry, in and by which untruths might be said, and even murder committed, without sin. Pardons and indulgences, on whatever pious reasons at first put forward, became at last purchasable means of committing sin, by escaping Church censure or purgatorial expiations; the teaching, as usual, was entirely lost sight of, that only the *saved* ever got so far as purgatory even! In fact, be a Christian, be a Romanist, was the sole teaching of Christendom during the middle ages, under Papal dominion.

Long after Rome had, as an empire, ceased to govern the world, she claimed, by her spiritual distinction, that which in former ages she had obtained alone by the function and authority of the empire. Under Constantine the Church was established with the State, which she cast off by degrees as she was tempted to become powerful in this world, and ultimately to become one of the kingdoms thereof. The services, ever since the amazing additions of Gregory I., and his commands to offer all public prayer in the Roman language, were calculated more for the aggrandisement of the papal religion than the Christian. And although, from the period when Wickliffe died, the revival of the practice and rites of the primitive Church, as far as possible, and consistent with the changes of society, had been gradually gaining ground, yet it was a task for labouring ages. Religion, as far as regards the distinction between its real sense and that which wrapped it and externally exhibited it in worship and government, had latterly passed away. The doctrine of the Primitive Church, justification by faith, had been supplanted by that of human merit; the doctrines of original sin, man's inability in his fallen state to please God, the necessity of Divine grace in order to be acceptable to God, were supplanted by supererogatory works, capable of being effected by saints so called, and every sort of delusive teaching, upon papal indulgence and unlimited absolution. It matters not what learned Romanists thought, or still think of these things in their right intention, the multitude will never be subtle dialecticians enough, or desire to distinguish the nice

ferences between what is intended and not intended by certain acts of devotion. Such doctrines, however explained, are not believed by the mass of ignorant or deluded otherwise than their perverted imaginations feign for them, and eagerly search for. The homage due to God alone was nicely defined, and an inferior portion devoted to images, relics and pilgrimages. The impressions of religion were now no longer taught with a view to be productive of those feelings of justice and veracity without which all intercourse between a man and his neighbour must cease to be safe. Faithfulness, duty, and love, in the several relations of life, were preached as if best exercised in monastic vows, or for the Church, which was the substituted word for our Saviour. Mildness, charity, and compassion, were only existing in those who were obedient and faithful to Roman influences, and were not to be exercised towards any but the faithful. Sobriety and industry were inferior to lowly reverence for saints, relics, the Pope, and Rome.

Thus, very naturally, a protestantising spirit was from time to time rising up from "prophets, priests, and kings," not, however, branded with the title of heresy, as long as in any way, and by any means, acquiescence in the authority of Rome was not ignored.

Nowhere had the secularization and grossness of the Papal Court spread with greater rapidity and license than in Germany. Its emperors had been insulted — its provinces distracted by Italian intrigue — the battles and miseries of four hundred years had prepared the people, far more than any other nation, for extreme measures, when the appointed time should arrive. A hundred grievances were in 1523 presented at the Diet of Nuremberg, representing only a small portion of hereditary wrongs, which formed the subject of perpetual remonstrance to, and perpetual contempt from the Papal Court. Three years subsequently, the great contending parties under Luther, Melancthon, Carlostadt, and all who agreed with them, were separated from the rest of the Papal governed people, by an arrangement arrived at in the Diet of Spires, which left the reforming states free to regulate their ecclesiastical affairs until a general council could be called together. Luther, however, had already been excommunicated by the Pope because he refused submission to Cardinal Cajetan, and to whatever the Cardinal might choose to expunge from the written views of Luther.

The mystery of iniquity, be it what it may, had begun to work in the apostolic times by a system of error; idolatry and intolerance gradually completed the full measure, in a desire for pre-eminence and love of this present world. When a power was to appear which had been prophesied " as that wicked, who opposeth and exalteth himself above all that is called God, or that is worshipped, so that he, as God, sitteth in the temple, showing himself that he is God," then must sacred Scripture be obeyed, which cries, " Come out of her my people." The revival of learning, and the art of printing, were, in their measure, some of the means which Providence saw fit to use in the bringing about a return to the old paths. The Papal schism, the violence of Anti-popes in excommunicating each other, the *necessary words* used by Councils when they were called to legislate upon the lives of the clergy, and indulgences, were so many awful revelations of depravity, and were, humanly speaking, the methods used by the Spirit to cry, " Come out of her."

In the beginning of the year 1517, Luther met Tetzel, the messenger of the Papal government, openly selling indulgences. The violence and impudence of Tetzel excited the equally violent temper and determination of Luther, who became the champion of the Reformation, by publishing ninety-five propositions against these indulgences. The Pope's summons to Luther to appear at Rome was overruled by the Elector of Saxony, and subsequently he was ordered to appear at Augsburg, where he held several conferences with Cardinal Cajetan. Luther appealed to the Pope, and returned to Wittemberg. In the meantime, Leo the Tenth published an edict which asserted his power to exempt from punishment due to all sins, or any sin. Luther instantly appealed to a General Council, upon which Leo excommunicated Luther. On the 10th of December 1520, with that wonted violence of character which alone could carry a reformer through the trials of that age, and which, had Berenger ages ago possessed, would have left less work for Luther, he burnt under the walls of Wittemberg the bull by which he had been excommunicated. At first Luther never — evidently from what has come down to us of his writings — intended going to the length circumstances subsequently led him, as they would have done any leader of reformation. To denounce the Pope as the " Man of Sin," was as much assuming himself to be infallible, in the interpretation of Scripture, as it would be in any other mortal. Melancthon, Zuinglius, and Calvin, ultimately associated themselves in the work which, from his domineering force of character, chiefly fell to Luther.

It is useless and foolish to judge of the Reformers by the measure and spirit of modern times ; in those dark ages in which Luther laboured, doubtless his mission and temper had much to endure. Nor would his object be met with that kind of forbearance in language or manners which alone could gain respect in modern days. Luther, though in genius and learning somewhat inferior to Calvin, was as far above him in the breadth and scope of his ideas, as in courage and force of character. In the States of Brandenburgh, Saxony, and Hesse, in the majority of what were called the imperial cities, in Sweden and in Denmark, shortly after the Diet of Spires in 1529, the Church reformed herself with varied degrees of success, and unfortunately, in the desire to escape one extreme, ran into the opposite, denying primitive usage, and every traditional circumstance of ritual which had been hallowed by the experience of the good and just for many ages. In 1530, Luther and Melancthon presented a Confession of their Faith, which was received under the name of the Augsburg Confession. In the month of December of the same year, the Princes of the Reforming Church assembled at Smalcald, entering into a league, known by that name in history, in which they agreed to unite and defend their common cause. In all this, nothing was done but by council and general agreement of the Church, and those who were her voice. It is, nevertheless, to be ever regretted, that man-made doctrines from that time, had a license and latitude approaching very much to an evil as great as when Popes disseminated novel views, from age to age, as circumstances dictated, or seemed to demand. Yet it were folly to deny, amid all and every sort of corruption in doctrine and ritual, that much true religion of the heart, which may and does consist with error in outward things, ripened into full maturity in many glorious characters which proceeded forth from the bosom of the Roman Church at that time. Doubtless the reforming spirit alarmed even Rome, so that by the time it had proceeded towards the south from the north, she had in many ways, and chiefly through such Christian characters as Francis Xavier, Borromeo, Archbishop of Milan, Francis de Sale, and others, lessened the opportunity for the Reformers to make way, especially in those countries where they would, from the nature of circumstances, appear in the character of disturbers of the temporal government. The Synod of Trent reformed some of the grosser abuses, but its Canons of discipline were not universally received. Bossuet and Veron, in their arguments, though opposing the protesting spirit of Reformation in the Christian Church, yet produced sounder and more moderate views on many subjects in the Roman Catholic Church which unhappily came now too late to save her. The struggle had begun in fact from the period of the Papal division, and the contests between the Councils of Pisa, Constance, and Basle, in the early part of the fifteenth century, and when the study of the Greek and Hebrew languages gradually led to the neglect of the scholastic writers.

It is always to be regretted that the Reformation was opposed by Rome from shame and anger, or it would have been promoted and regulated by the whole Church, by Councils and decrees of Synods. The "good seed" is still choked and overwhelmed by many tares, which arose " while men slept," yet now no one need live in gross error, though at this period, and all periods, no purity of religious forms, no Church, however pure, can cause men to live without impurity, imperfection, and sin—a heritage descended from age to age to man, among the blessings of Gospel light, and the gifts of sacramental grace conveyed in and by the Reformed Church.

QUESTIONS.

What Pope increased the growing antipathy to the power of the Papacy?

What was the nature of the disputes between France and the Pope in the beginning of the 14th century?

What daring act of Philip of France betokened a change of opinion as to the Papal authority?

What was the statute of Præmunire? What was that of Mortmain?

What were "annates," and when abolished?

What were the antecedents of the Pragmatic Sanction of Leo X.?

What detailed oppressions of the Church of England were questions in the 13th century?

Who was Grostete?

Who was Sewell of York and Richard of Chester?

What did they assert?

What index of change in public opinion arose now?

Was Wickliffe a means of expressing opinions already existing?

Who probably spread abroad his works and views?

Who was Huss? Was he a zealous Romanist Reformer?

How did he acknowledge the Papal authority?

What did he anticipate?

What concession was granted to the laity at the Council of Iglau?

Who were the United Brethren?

What opinions gained ground since the death of Wickliffe?

What doctrines were severally opposed by erroneous teaching in the Church?

Why is all explanation of what a superstition means rightly, useless to the morality of the people?

To be Christian had merged into what fact?

Why had Rome claimed universal dominion?

Who first commanded the services to be said in Latin?

What were the "hundred grievances?"

L

What was gained to reforming states at the Diet of Spires?

What was religious teaching actually opposed to in the 16th century?

What acts were favourable to reforming views?

In what year did Tetzel publicly sell indulgences?

What propositions did Luther publish?

To whom did Luther appeal after conferring with Cardinal Cajetan?

What public announcement of Leo forced Luther to appeal to a General Council?

Wherein did Luther differ from a former Reformer?

In what way did Luther expose his weakness?

In what spirit ought we *not to judge* the Reformers?

Give some account of Calvin?

Who presented the Augsburg Confession, and when?

What was the League of Smalcald?

What is to be regretted from this point of history?

What is due to the Church of Rome?

Why did not reforming views spread farther south?

What holy characters influenced the times now?

What did the Synod of Trent effect? What did the study of the ancient languages effect?

Printed by BoD™in Norderstedt, Germany